FMA EDUCATION

Leopoldo,
Maraming Salamat po.
Mabuhay.

Dec. 10 2016

SANANO

FMA EDUCATION
The Fundamental Core of
ARNIS DE MANO

LOUELLE C. LLEDO, JR. | **ANDY T. SANANO, JR.**

TECHNICAL CONSULTANTS:

EMMANUEL ES QUERUBIN | JOSE N. SIDLACAN | DR. MARK WILEY

www.TambuliMedia.com
Spring House, PA USA

DISCLAIMER

First Published by Tambuli Media on November 25, 2016

ISBN-13: 978-0692815526
ISBN-10: 069281552X
Library of Congress Control Number: 2016950535

Copy Editor: Victoria Touati
Cover and Interior: Summer Bonne

TABLE OF CONTENTS

PART 2: PRINCIPLES OF CLASSICAL MANEUVERS

PART 3: EVOLUTION TO PROGRESSIVE TECHNIQUES

PART 4: THE PATTERNS OF FUNDAMENTAL TRAINING

PART 5: KARUNUNGANG LIHIM (KALI) NG ARNIS DE MANO

PART 6: SPORTS ARNIS TOURNAMENT RULES & REGULATIONS

FOREWORD

Louelle Lledo and Andy Sanano have taken on quite a task. To begin, they are attempting to pull their knowledge and experience into an education program for the arts of Arnis, which they refer to as FMA Education. And it truly is based in education, not in style. Let me explain.

There are thousands of techniques in FMA; too many to count and they continue to evolve as each practitioner gains more experience. And there are hundreds of styles, or personal expressions of FMA, many of which are steeped in some tradition as passed down for generations. Some masters share their style through showing students how to do this or that, in this way and in that way. Others have set up teaching curriculum to be followed to learn the art.

What Mataw Guros Lledo and Sanano have done is to correlate the techniques of FMA and create a basic standard of fundamentals that they hope all will embrace. You see, according to their research, there are a small set of "Classical Maneuvers" from which all techniques are based, and there are but two "Basic Strikes" from which all strikes derive. And so, if you can learn the basic maneuver and strikes as a foundation, then everyone will have the same strong basics to then progress their journey in the arts by entering a style. This FMA Education effort in no way is trying to push aside the vast styles or organizations promoting FMA. Rather, it is an offering, a set of basic training fundamentals from which a strong base in Arnis de Mano can be acquired and then build from in pursuit of a specific style or two.

This takes guts because not all styles use the same basics; and many even forego basic training in favor of techniques practice from day one. Well, I commend these gentlemen for their dedication, vision and mission. Their group, The Mataw Guro Association, is growing quickly through their FMA Education efforts. As a Senior Adviser to the Mataw Guro Association and Faculty Member of the Mataw Guro Academy, I commend and respect this and for that I am pleased to call these men my friends and to publish their book.

— Dr. Mark Wiley,
Publisher, Tambuli Media
President, Integrated Eskrima International
Senior Adviser, Mataw Guro Association

FOREWORD

There are basics to all Filipino martial arts, to put it in laymen's words, it is like creating a meal, one must start with the basic ingredients and build the meal from there.

Mataw-Guro Louelle Lledo Jr. who is the original practitioner that formed the Mataw-Guro Association, was conscious of the need of developing enthusiasm, interest and dedication in the field of Filipino Martial Arts Education, joined by Mataw-Guro Andy Sanano Jr. their desire is to establish an Association which would be the rallying point of all teachers of Arnis de Mano as a Filipino Martial Arts Education.

The Mataw-Guro Association was formed to merge the different styles and systems to design, established and approve a basic fundamental for teaching Filipino martial arts education, specially Arnis de Mano to be presented to the Philippine Government, Sports and Education Commission, as the Mataw-Guro Association contribution to the Arnis de Mano development, grassroots, schools, Colleges and Universities Physical Education Programs. It is based on the four classical or traditional systems common to all the different major styles of the Filipino martial arts in the Philippines.

In learning the fundamentals, concepts, and principles in this book one should be able to continue their training in any Filipino martial art with little difficulty in that the student would just have to adapt their knowledge and skill to the desired style concept, principles and beliefs.

From beginner to the most knowledgeable practitioner this book will be very beneficial in learning, for the beginner in understanding and being able to grasp the basics and for the experienced practitioner reviewing where it all starts.

—   Punong Guro Steven K. Dowd
       Publisher, *FMA Informative*
       Punong Guro at Tagapagmana, Arnis Balite

FOREWORD

To commence, as a Medical Advisor for the MGA International Academy, I would humbly like to thank Dr. Mark Wiley to consider me to write the Foreword for this current edition of the FMA Education Series written by two highly regarded and well versed Martial Arts Educators, MG Louelle Lledo, Jr. and MG Andy Sanano, Jr., in which I consider to be personal friends and training brothers.

My association with MG Lou began in Chinatown, NYC in 2002 where we exchanged experiences in a Martial Arts Supply Store and subsequently our friendship grew whereby we decided to combine our efforts and expertise forming Sword Stick Society International (SSSI) in 2005. This organization's Mission was modeled after the Society of Black Belts of America (SOBBA) founded in 1964 by my most influential mentor, GM Robert L. Murphy. It became a vehicle to present Continuing Educational Workshops to martial artists regardless of one's system, style or rank.

After the untimely passing of MG Mark Lledo in 2008, beloved son of MG Louelle Lledo, to continue the legacy of his martial arts family MG Lou formed the Mataw Guro Association in 2010 modeled after SSSI & SOBBA. Our anticipated FMA Gatherings where prominent Master Teachers shared their skills as a brother and sisterhood was when I formally met MG Andy Sanano.

As I followed the MGA through its natural growing pains, one thing is very clear, that their depth and breadth of vast knowledge is only second to their Passion and Compassion to eagerly Preserve, Promote & Perpetuate their experiences in the Military, Martial & Medical Field.

As professionals, and representatives of SOBBA, they have excelled in the Filipino and other Martial Arts respectfully while continually striving to polish and perfect their own abilities through a whole-hearted rigorous exchange of ideas.

Their openness and willingness to share, compare & contrast is a mirror of our times and is an invaluable asset in disparity to the not so distant past of secrecy.

Research and development of authentic indigenous Classical Maneuvers within FMA training methodology, whether obscure or mainstream, has given rise to the formation of this Teacher's Manual as the drills leading to skills are firmly rooted in a common language of Biomechanics based upon Anatomy & Physiology and Physics.

In this digital age of technology and social media ... constant access to FMA has never been easier and which was not available in just recent times. With that comes the chance to sift and sort through data scrutinizing every detail. However, with the broad spectrum of Systems and Styles available for the consumer ... one can easily become confused and misled.

With shorter attention spans and numerous distractions, the FMA practitioners, representatives and teachers of today and tomorrow need guideposts and secure stepping stones. Fortunately, MG Lledo's approach of "System of Systems", with the emphasis of refined basics found in this training manual is the common thread that binds all Systems.

This reference provides a clear, concise and organized approach of the fundamentals inherent in all FMA Education thus bringing together the many varied field-proven factions of blade, stick and empty hand theories & practices, reflecting a path to the hidden Wisdom within these precious FMA Martial Disciplines.

This valuable source of instruction and advisement is one answer to cultivate that Quest for Self-Preservation, Self-Development and Self-Mastery found in the many reasons for training ... Physical Well Being, Practical Martial Prowess, Mental Clarity, and Spiritual Cleansing Abilities.

This is where the Art Form of Self-Expression is born as the Warrior Scholar within emerges in this present generation and is cultivated in the generations to follow.

As another new Horizon arises ... we look forward to these seasoned writers for their follow-up topics and the reader's contributions as arrows in our ever-expanding quivers as we travel the enlightened Path of the Mandirigma.

— Dr. Christopher M. Viggiano
Medical Advisor, MGA International Academy
Director & CEO, Society of Black Belts of America
Founder & Headmaster, Shen Wu Dao Martial & Healing Arts
Co-Founder, Sword Stick Society International
Co-Founder, United Fellowship of Martial Artists

PREFACE

In 2009, Arnis de Mano was declared the official national martial art and sport of the Phillipines. The official rules and regulations for Arnis de Mano were created to establish a standard method of instruction so Arnis de Mano could be part of the curriculum for all grade levels in both public and private schools.

Unfortunately, several attempts to create official rules and regulations were unsuccessful. "Grandmasters" and "Masters" of different schools and styles were unwilling to compromise and agree on a standard method of instruction. They wanted their own system of teaching to be the model despite popular support of the Republic Act 9850 (see Appendix 1).

On February 27, 2011, Cavite State University, located in Indang, Cavite in the Phillipines, hosted an Arnis de Mano workshop and gathering. The subject of the workshop was "Filipino Martial Arts Education," based on the training handbooks of Louelle Lledo, Jr. and Andy Sanano, Jr., the authors of the combined-volume you are now reading.

Guests of honor in this workshop included the Honorable Senator Miguel Zubiri, author of the Republic Act 9850, better known as the "Arnis Law"; the Honorable Bienvenido Dimero, Mayor of Indang, Cavite; Dr. Davinia Chavez, President of the Cavite State University; Dr. Alejandro Mojica, Cavite State University Vice-President; and Dr. Alejandro Dagdag, Executive Director of the Integrated College of Physical Education and Sports. These last three guests of honor represented the academy.

The highlight of this event was the presentation of **"The Award for Meritorious Service to Philippine Culture,"** signed by Honorable Senator Miguel Zubiri and other guests to Louelle Lledo, Jr. and Andy Sanano, Jr. The award dedication reads:

"In recognition of their unrelenting and undying exemplary determination in the development, and propagation of Arnis de Mano as an ancient art, a science of self-preservation, a modern competitive sport and an integral part of Philippine history and culture."

Other major awards have been awarded to Louelle Lledo, Jr., and Andy Sanano, Jr.:

The Award of Excellence, for the Development, Propagation, and Promotion of the Filipino martial arts in the United States of America by the United Fellowship of Martial Artists in Philadelphia, PA.

The "Bukal ng Karunungan" (Fountain of Knowledge) award on April 14, 2012 by the Honorable Juanito Victor Remulla, Jr., governor of Cavite Province.

The Outstanding Volunteer Award in 2012 by President Barack Obama to Louelle Lledo, Jr. for his invaluable service in teaching Filipino martial arts to the non-commissioned officers of the U.S. Army stationed at Fort Dix, in New Jersey.

With almost 100 years of combined experience in teaching the martial arts, both armed and unarmed, the authors decided to document their proven method of instruction and co-wrote four separate educational manuals on the Filipino martial arts. The manuals were published and widely accepted. However, they received several requests to combine the separate manuals into one book, and this publication is the result.

As you go through this book, you may notice that some pictures, words, sentences, and phrases are repeated. For emphasis and continuity, the authors feel this was necessary. This repetition illustrates how "the whole is the sum of all the parts."

Our students and other practitioners who have followed the method of instruction in these manuals have been helped to become better arnisadors and teachers of Arnis de Mano. We hope you too will find this book helpful in your quest to master the Filipino martial art of Arnis de Mano.

There is a saying…

> *"Education is a movement from darkness to light.*
> *Martial arts education is a journey from ignorance to understanding."*

We invite all the martial artists to join us in this journey. Wishing you the best in your practice.

Louelle C. Lledo, Jr.
Amara Arkanis International

Andy T. Sanano, Jr.
Sanano Martial Arts System

PART I

FUNDAMENTALS OF ARNIS DE MANO

This teachers' training handbook is designed for current, prospective, and aspiring Filipino martial arts teachers and practitioners. It deals exclusively with the foundation of Arnis de Mano and how it should be taught to convey the underlying principles of every technique and maneuver. There are no "advanced" techniques in this handbook. The authors do not believe in advanced techniques. What others call advanced techniques are considerd basic techniques performed in a superior manner. In order to perform the maneuvers in a superior manner, the principle of MIBOME (MIndset and BOdy MEchanics) must be applied in a "simple reaction." The program of instruction is divided into five parts, as documented in this Section.

CHAPTER 1

BUILDING THE FOUNDATION

WHEN TO BEGIN TRAINING

There are two schools of thought on how early one should start physical training. One school advocates starting early because most successful athletes who achieve international success and fame or who possess the ability and skill for international competition have anywhere from five to 15 years of training and competing experience.

In most athletic events, athletic maturity is attained between the ages of 20 and 30. There are gifted ones who have extended their staying power to 40 years or even way past that age. Once in a while, there are exceptional athletes who stay on top of their sport even at the "ripe old" age of 50 years.

The "earlier the better" school of thought insists that it is good to instill the competitive spirit in the child at an early age. However, not every youngster has the inclination or discipline to achieve athletic fame. Those who are impressed by other athletes to be great and successful set a specific goal and work hard to perfect their style and technique even without outside influence. They work hard towards peak form and strive to improve and develop in every training session without being told to do so. Then there are some who train just for their own satisfaction and enjoyment.

"There is no better art, only a better man."

Most medical professionals agree that imparting the interest to participate in physical training at an early age is very good, not only for the health of the body, for the total well-being of the child.

The other school of thought does not encourage training at an early age and takes a more conservative, cautious approach. This school maintains that children below a certain age level still have underdeveloped motor skills, nervous systems, and muscle coordination. At this stage, the body is undergoing a lot of changes and adjustments. The body structure changes and a heavy and strict regimen of exercise is not advisable or practical. When the motor nerve is still in the developmental stage, it is very easy to develop bad habits and "out of sync" techniques, which may be difficult to correct later on.

"If you hear you forget. If you see, you remember. If you do, you learn."

On account that not everyone is the same, the best gauge in how early martial arts training should start must be the youngster's reaction, enthusiasm, enjoyment and individual development. Stimulate the child to have fun and enjoy the training as a game. However, even at the early stages of a youngster's training, correct procedure and good form must be emphasized at all times and must take precedence over speed and power.

The medical field may always be divided on this matter, but Filipino martial arts education programs must be designed with practitioners of all ages in mind. The program must be basic enough for youngsters to understand and enjoy, yet progressive enough for advanced students to attain superior performance.

On the other end of the spectrum, there is no maximum age limit to start and engage in martial arts training. Age may be a factor in competition. However, there are some tournaments where there are age classifications all the way up to the senior years. Age is not a factor that will prevent an individual, no matter what gender, to participate in any physical activity. Scientific studies have proven that health may be improved even by the simplest physical activity as walking. Martial arts training involves a complete body mechanics of bodily exertion that develops and maintains physical fitness. The program in this handbook is appropriate even for a geriatric or wheelchair bound individual. An individual who no longer needs or wants to engage in the combat aspect of martial arts may still feel the adrenalin flowing through as they complete drills and hit the heavy bag or a similar training aid.

APEX AND MIBOME

In television journalism classes, the writer is taught to use the inverted pyramid method to cover stories. In the inverted pyramid, the beginning of a story contains the majority of the content – the widest part – and the ending of the story contains the smallest amount of details – the narrowest part:

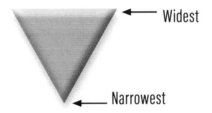

Journalism's Inverted Pyramid

Using the inverted pyramid method, the writer provides an overview of the story's main points at the very beginning including the characters involved, where the story took place, how it took place, and why it took place. The rationale is that the audience gets the main points of the story right away, regardless of how much is modified or altered by the editor.

In martial arts, the inverted triangle is reversed. The bottom is the widest part and the top is the narrowest part. The widest part is called the foundation and the narrowest part is called the apex. Even if you were to cut the top off, you'd still have a wide base to fall back on.

In Filipino martial arts, the student is advised to select the best technique (Apex) based on their foundation.

Based On Your Foundation Select The Best Technique For You (Apex)

Foundation - The Widest (MIBOME)

Martial Arts Pyramid

The apex is the culmination of doing the basic techniques a thousand times based on the principle of Mindset and Body Mechanics (MIBOME). The principles and techniques of MIBOME involve breath-control, stance, center of gravity, footwork, transfer of motion, efficiency, consistency of movement, balance, distance, timing, focus, direct application of force and leverage, which equates to one's simple reaction. MIBOME is the collective term for spirit, skill, speed, strength, and style.

MIBOME equates to good form, which is sometimes defined as "economy of motion." A good teacher will teach that best performance is achieved through striving for the best form possible, which corresponds to minimum use of motion and wasted energy, but maximum efficiency. Energy saved by sound "mechanics of form" translates into a more forceful expression of the skill. Practitioners must always attempt to exert all the momentum in the effective direction, while not forgetting that one "form" may be suitable for one athlete, but impractical for another. Applying the MIBOME approach to your martial arts practice helps improve and achieve the following results:

- Variation of force and speed, which is essential for the various movement of a skill pattern.

- Timing of movements in the pattern and the complete pattern.

- The effective use of physical principles of leverage in connection with the projection of force, inertia, and momentum.

- Concealment of intent from the opponent.

- Beauty of motion. The principles of beauty in sports are no different from the principles of beauty in art or architecture.

- Proper footwork. Footwork makes direct lines of force possible, initiation of movement easier, and increase the possible range of motion.

- More precise control over one's center of gravity.

- Individuality in form. Instead of imitating others, which limits one's potential by what he imitates; an individual must develop a form that is truly his own.

- Ambidexterity or the skilled use of either hand or foot for a movement pattern.

- Follow-through or an acceleration of recognition of a threat to the completion of the application of the technique in neutralizing the threat.

Martial arts are similar to constructing a building. You always start from the bottom. The bigger and taller the building, the wider and sturdier the foundation must be. There should be more piles driven and they should be driven deep to make a solid foundation and hold the weight of the building. The rationale is the stronger and sturdier the foundation, the stronger and more effective the technique will be. As stated earlier, this handbook deals exclusively with the basic techniques, the fundamentals of the art that form the very foundation of mastery. To the uninitiated and to those who do not or refuse to understand, it must be emphasized there are no advance techniques only basic techniques that are executed in a superior manner. Likewise, there are no blocks in Arnis de Mano, only defensive courses of action. Strikes are used not to block or stop an attack, but to deflect and re-direct the attack. As the student progresses, he will understand. People who have witnessed practitioners perform the intricate swirling of the sticks may

> "Strikes are used not to block or stop an attack, but to deflect and re-direct the attack. As the student progresses, he will understand."

say that is what they want to learn. They may even say they do not want to be bothered with the basic techniques or they do not have the time or they just want to learn how to fight. To these people, all that can be said is they do not understand that martial arts training is about more than swinging limbs and weapons in a flashy way.

This teachers' training handbook is designed for current, prospective, and aspiring martial arts teachers or practitioners who want to understand the Filipino martial arts concepts of effective teaching and learning. The material is systematically arranged so as to make the student aware of each technique's specific application in the overall scheme of things. For the most efficient mastery of concepts, each technique is broken down into its most basic elements and minute skills. For example, stick fighting is a complex skill. In learning a complex skill, one must begin with a framework towards a goal, with a complete and thorough understanding of the principles involved in each movement.

Regardless of religious orientation, one cannot deny that duality of nature is the hallmark of creation. There is always a beginning and an end; the sky and the earth; up and down; right and left; male and female. Stick fighting is the same thing, as explained below:

- There are only two patterns of motion: *linear* and *circular.*
- There are only two types of strikes: *forehand* and *backhand.*
- There are only two types of thrusts: *overhand* and *underhand.*
- There are only two empty-hand disarm maneuvers: *turn* and *twist.*
- There are two actions that off-balance the opponent: *push* and *pull.*
- There are only two opposing forces: *centrifugal* and *centripetal.*
- There are two principles that govern every maneuver: *efficiency* and *consistency.*

To explain the last point, efficiency is accomplishing a specific goal in as little time and with as little effort as possible, while consistency is executing the technique the same, correct way every time.

By developing the techniques that work best for you based on your training and physical capability and then limiting the mechanical and mental options until "simple reaction" is achieved, consistent efficiency and efficient consistency may be attained as the very top or apex of the martial arts pyramid.

To those who do not understand or refuse to understand, look at all the swirling and twirling of the sticks; they are nothing more than the forehand or backhand strikes, the overhand or underhand thrust executed in linear or circular motions. This also illustrates why martial arts teaching must be systematically arranged. Pile driving and solid preparation of the foundation must be achieved prior to putting the roof on and the walls up.

The pre-requisite requirement for taking this course is a basic skill in Arnis de Mano and an open mind to understand the lessons thoroughly.

TRAINING OBJECTIVES

This handbook is designed to help you plan programs to teach the Filipino martial arts of Anis de Mano. Although all the lessons in this handbook are also practical for live blades, swords, knives, other alternative weapons or even empty hands, the main scope is the use of double sticks or *doble baston*. The use of double sticks is not only encouraged but also mandatory in learning Arnis de Mano in order to develp ambidexterity and avoid becoming a one-sided fighter.

Defensive and offensive techniques in Filipino martial arts revolve in a pentagonal foundation (known as MIBOME) that are interrelated and complement each other in spirit, skill, speed, strength and style, as follows:

Spirit—Spirit is the mental aspect. It is the active type of utmost concentration in every aspect of training. For clarity, spirit will be referred to as "active meditation." It has nothing to do with religion or spirituality; although it is similar in the sense that the aim is "oneness of mind and body." This "state of oneness" is possible only with rigid training and strict discipline in accepting the martial arts as a way of life and not just a combative art.

Skill—Before speed and strength, a student must have the ability to hit the intended target with the proper weapon at the proper time. In simple terms, this is called accuracy or precision of movement. It is also known as exactness of the projection of force. To achieve this aspect, the student must be taught the proper sequence in muscle contraction and relaxation, timing, balance, distance, coordination and most important of all: breath control. This type of training makes the student focus more directly on a situation and elicits a more rapid response. Every aspect of learning is an active process that teaches a student to apply a simple reaction. A simple reaction is faster than a choice reaction.

Speed—Through training, the practitioner learns that speed comes not from moving faster, but from the efficiency of the movement. Efficiency of movement includes the time of recognizing the threat up to the time of neutralizing the threat. This ability of "recognition and reaction" is attainable only through proper and constant training. Every technique, both defensive and offensive, must be executed in natural rhythm with minimal effort based on the underlying principle that a simple state creates speed, and a fluid response generates maximum speed, and maximum speed achieves maximum efficiency.

Strength—Big muscles that are needed to move heavy objects at a slow rate of time play a secondary role in Filipino martial arts. Sinewy, flexible muscles that can move a lighter weight at a greater speed are more important. In martial arts, strength may be better represented as power. Power is generated not by brute force, but through efficiency of movement and directness of application of energy. As a natural simple state creates speed, it also creates power. Sometimes power is also defined as "explosiveness," created by muscle-speed unification or muscle contraction of every part of the body at a given instant. All techniques in martial arts must be designed to offer all around development by utilizing the principle of motion and applying the best angle of force.

Style—No two human beings are exactly alike psychologically or physiologically. In order to achieve maximum results, a technique must be executed according to an individual's physical capability. The art must be adapted to the practitioner, not the other way around. The system is based on the principle that the simpler the technique, the more effective it is. An attribute of style is form. Good form is an important aspect of the martial arts. Best results are achieved through good form. Good form creates proper muscle tension and contraction, which in turn minimizes wasted energy. Good form also facilitates movement because it affords better control of the center of gravity and balance. Good form is a manifestation of a properly directed energy that results in superior performance. Do not imitate others or your form will be limited by what you see and imitate. Study and learn the techniques, improve on them, and develop your own form based on your own physical capability.

MINDSET

The dictionary defines mindset as attitude. It is also defined as state or frame of mind. There are those who call it determination or motivation. Others use more colorful terms such as "never say die" or "do-or-die" and other descriptive terms. For our purpose, we will simply call it *mindset*.

More than good technique, and more than proper conditioning, mindset is the most important factor in any encounter. A fighter less skilled and less conditioned but possessing the proper mindset can beat an opponent who does not have the appropriate mindset.

There are individuals born with a positive mindset who are ready and willing to face any type of confrontation head on. These people have self-confidence, self-reliance and the determination to be steadfast.

"There are those born with a negative mindset and hide their weakness behind the cloak of pacifism. They mistake timidity and fear for peace and even godliness.

Unfortunately, there are those born with a negative mindset and hide their weakness behind the cloak of pacifism. They mistake timidity and fear for peace and even godliness. They mistake docile submission as cooperative endeavor, not realizing or perhaps refusing to admit that it means crushed spirits and unhealthy attitudes.

Opposition to the use of force under any circumstances may be a noble ideal but in the real world where "dog eats dog," it may cost an individual his or her life or the life of a loved one. It is an individual's right and duty to protect and defend oneself and his or her loved ones against harm and violence.

Skill in any fighting art in itself may not alter an individual's mindset because mindset comes from within the individual. However, martial arts may build self-confidence. This self-confidence may help the individual turn fear into an unwavering and resolute spirit, the main ingredients of a positive mindset.

Self-confidence and self-reliance create a positive mindset. With this frame of mind, an individual is ready and willing to stand straight and face the world head up high against adversity. Positive mindset in itself is a firm strategy.

A positive mindset must not be confused with haphazard aggressive action. A positive mindset is the product of proper training. A well trained mind cannot be overwhelmed by fear or defeat. A well trained mind will enable an individual to execute techniques and maneuvers without consciously thinking about it. In this state of mind, an individual will have no doubt or hesitation. With a positive mindset, the inner self (mind) and the outer self (body) work together in harmony.

It is sometimes possible to diffuse hostile intent when you project an aura of self-confidence. Sometimes, though, you may have to take a more positive and proactive step when an antagonistic attitude portends an impending confrontation. In this type of situation, you must always take advantage of your opponent's initial move. Aside from the motivation of avoiding being struck, you must have the willingness to strike back, strike hard and strike effectively, and completely neutralize the threat. Some even claim that the "taste of blood" only makes them bolder and stronger.

Proper training will give you the ability to gauge your opponent's intentions. Proper training will enable you to form strategies against an opponent's attack. When your opponent takes the initiative to strike first, proper training will enable you to avoid being struck by striking your opponent faster and harder. Do not allow your opponent to recover from your strike. Do not take it for granted that once you hit your opponent, you must discontinue your attack. Do not dwell on your first strike or it will lose its effectiveness. Keep on striking and never give your opponent a chance to gain his composure. If your opponent is as skillful as you are, shift your strategy. Use broken-timing and never give your opponent the opportunity to figure out your rhythm. Always keep your opponent off-balance. Always strive to end the confrontation with one strike, and, if possible, the first strike. After all, the Filipino martial arts is based on the principle of "one-strike, one-kill." All these put together is what a positive mindset is all about.

> "The difference between offense and defense is only a perception."

Mindset makes the difference when the requirement is beyond the common experience.

TEACHER OR INSTRUCTOR?

In the English language, the terms teacher and instructor are used interchangeably and are synonymous. In Filipino, these terms are both translated as *guro.* However, in Filipino, the term teacher is normally used in an educational institution, and carries a deeper meaning. A teacher builds character and attitude. A teacher invokes virtues that make a good individual great.

In martial arts, the term commonly used is instructor. An instructor drills students in techniques and maneuvers. An instructor's goal is to make a better practitioner of a particular system or art, like the drill instructor in the military.

In martial arts, the term that *must* be used is *teacher.* A teacher teaches an individual, not only to be a good fighter, but more important to be a better person; a fighter, who not only can execute the techniques skillfully, but also understand how the technique can be skillfully executed. The teacher helps mold the student into a fighter who can execute a maneuver with minimum effort but with maximum result. A teacher must be a technician of skill and a designer of growth and development.

A teacher must cultivate the student's mind, not only to be excellent in the performance of the techniques, but also to be an exceptional strategist. The teacher must always impart to the student the desire to strive for perfection by diligent and constant training, and to endeavor to build a solid foundation, both mentally and physically. A teacher must instill in the student the importance of accurate performance rather than just a demonstration of power. A teacher must teach individuality of behavior.

Learning is much easier than teaching the fighting arts. To be a teacher, one must have mastered the art at a level that must be greater than ordinary. Having learned the art, one must be able to put the techniques into practice and believe in what he teaches. Finally, one must be able to realize and work on an individual's characteristics and learning habits.

> "Do one technique a thousand times rather than one thousand techniques one time."

A teacher must understand and master the principles and the techniques himself and then be able to impart this knowledge and mastery to the student. The teacher must always remember that teaching is also a process of learning.

Patience is a virtue that all teachers must possess and practice. Not all students have the same learning ability. There are students that are fast learners and naturally gifted. There are students that are slow and awkward. A teacher must always base the techniques on correct principles, no matter how uncoordinated the student may be. The teacher must adapt the art to the physical limitation of the student. The teacher who follows this attitude will himself make great progress in the techniques he is teaching. A teacher must constantly strive for correct progress.

A teacher must not try to stand out by showing off his strength or skills. Strength and skills are different from being a good teacher. It is very desirable to be technically skillful and to be a good teacher at the same time, but sometimes a teacher may not be skillful at the techniques himself, but can successfully teach others to be skillful. Sometimes, a practitioner may be very skillful but cannot successfully teach others, making him unqualified to be a teacher.

A good teacher must not teach students to imitate techniques alone, but make the student understand the techniques with bodily movements that conform to the correct principles. By striving and devising a system to teach a slow learner, the teacher develops discipline and leadership in the basic principles and finer points of his art.

A good teacher must have the genius to bring out the students' talents and abilities. He does not need to justify or promote his actions. He must be respected and not feared by his students.

A good teacher must always motivate his students to strive for superior performance and be able to unleash all of the student's physiological and psychological reserve of energy at the right instance.

Teachers are committed, not only in teaching the techniques, but in enlightening the mind and nurturing the spirit of the student.

A student's spirit is a mirror image of the teacher. If the teacher has a humble spirit, the student likewise will have a humble spirit. If the teacher is conceited, the student will also be conceited. A mediocre teacher produces a mediocre student; a good teacher produces good students; and, an excellent teacher produces an excellent student. Conversely, an excellent student brings out the excellence in a teacher.

Teacher as First Responder

It would be ideal if every martial arts teacher knew what to do when suddenly confronted with an emergency. In reality, they look to others who are more knowledgeable to care for an injured person. However, in a life or death situation, waiting for more advanced medical personnel may not be ideal or timely. Since you are the teacher and presumably the person in authority, you must be the first trained professional to take responsibility at the scene of an emergency.

Many people fail to give emergency care due to concern about lawsuits. However, since you are the teacher, it is your duty to give a certain standard of care to your student or you may be guilty of negligence. Negligence includes acting wrongly or failing to act at all. As the teacher, you have a duty to act in a life-threatening emergency.

Places that have Good Samaritan laws protect people who provide emergency care. It is imperative that as the teacher, you are aware of the laws related to emergency care since they may be different from city to city, state to state, and country to country.

> *"A good teacher must have the genius to bring out the students' talents and abilities. He does not need to justify or promote his actions. He must be respected and not feared by his students."*

Always maintain a caring and professional attitude, and ensure your own safety and the safety of bystanders. An individual has a basic right to decide what can and cannot be done to his or her body. When possible, you must first obtain the person's consent for treatment, whether actual or implied. Implied consent is when the person is unconscious, severely injured, confused or is a minor and obviously needing emergency care when a parent or a guardian is not present. Even when a person is severely injured, he or she has the right to refuse emergency care. Another thing to keep in mind is the victim's right to privacy by maintaining confidentiality about the care you gave with the exception of sharing this information with law enforcement or other medical personnel caring for the victim.

It is preferred for martial arts teachers to be first aid certified or familiar with how to handle the following life threatening emergencies in class:

1. How to apply cardio-pulmonary resuscitation (CPR).
2. How to stop bleeding
3. How to stabilize the neck and the spine

For non-life-threatening injuries, teachers should be prepared to take the following steps:

1. Make the victim as comfortable as possible
2. Apply appropriate first aid
3. Seek medical advice and assistance if needed

Dr. Chris Viggiano, Senior Adviser of the Mataw Guro Association and President of the Society of Black Belts of America, also suggests knowing if any of the students is taking medication for health concerns that may turn into an emergency. He further suggests making sure the student has the medication readily available while training, and that the teacher knows when and how to properly dispense the medication. The student's record must also provide an emergency contact or the student's physician on file.

Note: Do not attempt emergency care above and beyond your ability and training.

Part of the mission of the martial arts teacher is to help avoid, prepare, respond, and cope with emergencies, and improve their students' quality of life by enhancing self-reliance and concern for others.

CHAPTER 2

GETTING STARTED

TRAINING ATTIRE

Training attire, most commonly referred to as a training uniform, must always allow for the freest possible movement of the body. It should also be conducive to the weather and allow the body to "breathe."

Unlike many other martial arts, Arnis de Mano does not have compulsory training attire. This is because in the early days of Arnis de Mano, training was done in secret. A teacher normally has just one student whom he teaches in the backyard, hidden from prying eyes.

The popularity of Arnis de Mano, specifically in the movies, resulted in the proliferation of commercial schools and gyms. With the enactment of the law declaring Arnis de Mano as the official national martial arts and sport in the Phillipines, more schools have mushroomed. Arnis de Mano is taught in both public and private schools. It is now the most prominent physical education curriculum. It is only a matter of time when a dress code will become a part of the training.

"One picture is better than a thousand words."

Commercial clubs have fancy uniforms for identification and advertising purposes. Some uniforms are military looking while some are plain but colorful (normally black and red) t-shirts with the name and logo of the club.

Whatever the style, color or type, club uniforms instill the feeling of importance and belonging. Likewise, it calls attention to the club and arouses the desire to be a part of the group. More important, a training uniform excites and stimulates an individual to action and to shift gears to a psychological readiness for activity. Even for these reasons alone, having a standard training uniform is advisable.

Students must all have the same training uniform, be it a simple white or same color t-shirt, and same color shorts or jogging pants. It is also advisable that the teacher's uniform be different from the students so he will stand out as being the leader. Training in uniforms give the student a sense of belonging to a particular mission like soldiers in the military.

Part of the training attire is the footwear. Inside the gymnasium where the floor is smooth and clean, training barefoot may be allowed. However, the teacher and all the students must be barefooted. Training outdoors is different. For health and safety reasons, appropriate footwear must be worn at all times. Like the training uniform, footwear must all be the same color, and, if possible, the same type, and either low cut or high cut.

> "Keep an open mind. You may learn something even from the dull and ignorant."

In the progressive stage, "real world attire" must also be part of the training. This is to offer "real world" situations. For police officers or military personnel, training while in their prescribed uniform with all the proper paraphernalia and equipment is a must.

SALUTATION

The old forms of *bigay galang* (showing respect) in the Filipino tradition is by removing the *balanggot* (native hat made of leaves or sheathing) for men and the *salakot* (native wide-brimmed head covering made of leaves or bamboo) or *pandong* (scarf covering the head) for women. For people with a difference in age, the custom is the *mano po* (your hand please), wherein the youngster reaches out for the elder's right hand and places it on the youngster's forehead at the same time uttering the words *mano po*.

When Spain colonized the Philippines, they introduced genuflecting on one knee and kissing the hand of the priest, friar or the influential, rich officials. The Americans brought with them the handshake and the "pat" on the back. In the short time Japan ruled over the Philippines, the tipping of the head in a bow was introduced as a sign of respect and salutation.

Pagpugay (salutation or bow) is a recent development in Arnis de Mano. In the old Arnis de Mano, when the art became a "sport contest," all the combatants would simply face each other, and, with an agreed signal, start the match. After the fight, the only salutation if there was any, was a polite *salamat po* (thank you).

In martial arts, the first lesson is demonstrating respect by the proper salutation. Contrary to some people's contentions, salutation is not a sign of subservience or obsequious servility, but a sign of respect, an expression of greeting, goodwill or courtesy by word, gesture or ceremony.

Bow by placing the stick to the forehead and saying, "I search for knowledge." The stick is then moved down to the right side as you say, "I show my respect." Then move the stick to the left side of the chest, saying "I pledge my loyalty." Now cross sticks in front of the lower body, saying "I'm ready for instruction." The teacher then turns and bows to class.

Presently, martial arts practitioners acknowledge each other by the *nakatayong pagpugay* (standing salutation), and the appropriate term of title as follows:

- *Kasama* (associate)
- *Bantas* (junior in grade, rank or standing)
- *Mantas* (senior in grade, rank or standing) or *Guro* (teacher)
- *Punong-guro* (head teacher)
- *Matawguro* (master teacher) *or*
- *Pantas* (grandmaster) followed by a guttural "po"

There is still no universal method of salutation in Arnis de Mano. The different schools have different ways. Some schools do not even teach the salutation. It is important to have a salutatory sign of respect before and after every training session.

BREATHING METHODS

Better breathing results in better performance. Proper breathing in the martial arts or any physical activity is of utmost importance. Breathing and performance go hand-in-hand. However, most instructors of the Filipino martial arts have relegated breathing to the background. Some have even totally ignored teaching proper breathing altogether. In martial arts, proper breathing should be the first priority.

> *"Breathing and performance go hand-in-hand. In martial arts, proper breathing should be the first priority."*

A long, vigorous, calm, smooth breath suggests a person is healthy. A weak, spasmodic, arbitrary breath suggests a weak, sickly person. Watch a healthy baby breathe while asleep. The lower abdomen goes up and down while the chest and shoulders remain calm. This is how one must strive to breathe.

Breathing may be simply defined as inhalation (taking air in) and exhalation (expelling air out). In martial arts, it may sound a little more complicated. Inhalation is drawing the universal energy into your body, forging that energy in your personal anvil of training, and expelling it out as a destructive or constructive force depending on the need and intention.

"If you want anything done right, do it yourself."

The normal flow of breathing is when you inhale during the preparatory stage, drawing all your training and preparation in your mind and body and then you exhale at the execution of the maneuver, concentrating all your mental energy and physical strength on the technique.

There are two major types of breathing in the martial arts. The first type of breathing is peaceful, meditative breathing that calms the spirit. This is done by inhaling through the nose and exhaling through the nose. Both inhalation and exhalation are done slowly, silently, and deeply. In inhalation, direct all the air down towards your lower abdomen. Hold it for as long as you comfortably can then expel all the air out. When you feel you have expelled all the air out, force one last exhalation also through the nose. This type of breathing is done during the period of meditation. Try to breathe this way every time.

The second type of breathing is dynamic breathing that strengthens the body. This type of breathing is done by inhaling through the nose and exhaling through the mouth. Inhalation is done slowly, silently, and deeply. When you inhale, direct all the air down towards your lower abdomen. Hold it for as long as you comfortably can and then expel all the air out through the mouth. At the culmination of the concentrated power, force one last exhalation forcefully and loudly (called *bunyaw*) from the lower abdomen and create the sound *t-s-a-h*. This breathing is normally used during drills and the application of techniques or whenever you exert effort. The *bunyaw* also tends to dampen the fighting spirit of the opponent.

Then, there is a type of breathing in which you inhale through the mouth and exhale through the mouth. This creates a shallow breathing and is typically known as "out of breath" breathing. When you breathe in this manner, it will be almost impossible to concentrate your energy. Therefore, this method is not one useful to martial arts.

Meditative Breathing Exercise

1. Stand in a natural, parallel stance with feet hip distance and hands hanging by your sides
2. Inhale through the nose as you turn palms upward slowly bringing them up to chest level
3. Inhale as you bring your hands up to chest level
4. Direct the air down towards the lower abdomen
5. Hold your breath as long as you comfortably can
6. Turn palms down and exhale through the nose as you bring your hands down. Exhaling and bringing the hands down must coincide and conclude at the same time.
7. Force one last exhalation through the nose
8. Hold breath for about one second
9. Repeat the up and down process five times

Note: When doing this meditative breathing exercise, it is advisable to keep the eyes closed. Settle your mind at the center of gravity and keep the body still. This exercise may be done standing up, sitting down or even kneeling.

Dynamic Breathing Exercise

1. Stand with feet spread hip width apart and your knees slightly bent and tensed outwards. Point your toes directly forward. Turn your palms up you're your elbows close to the body.
2. Execute a double, middle, outward open-hand block with palms facing you as you inhale silently, smoothly and deeply through the

nose directing the air to the lower abdomen.

3. Hold your breath for as long as you comfortably can.

4. Execute a middle, outward, open-hand block with palms facing forward as you exhale through your mouth (forcing air out like blowing into a balloon), tucking your buttocks in, pressing shoulders down and tensing abdominal and side muscles

5. Force one last exhalation through your mouth.

6. Hold breath for about one second.

7. Repeat the process five times.

Warm Up and Cool Down

To avoid injury and get the maximum benefit of any physical activity, a good warm up and cool down period is necessary. The more intense the workout, the harder the warm up must be. All of the body must be sufficiently warmed up before heavy training requiring speed, strength or both is performed. Likewise, the body must cool down slowly after a heavy workout to give the muscles enough time to return to its natural state. Warm up and cool down exercises are based on the same fundamental principles, but differ in emphasis and purpose. Proper breathing is a very important part of warm up and cool down exercises.

Warm up exercises (usually calisthenics) allow the muscles to receive the blood and oxygen required for the actual workout. A good warm up exercise to start with is jumping jacks or jogging in place. These exercises should be done slowly but with rhythm to ensure that blood circulates properly. Stretching exercises must also be part of a warm-up routine. Stretching the muscles makes them flexible and less susceptible to injury.

It is also advisable to select specific stick-fighting exercises during non-training days to improve skill and performance, and to keep the muscles limber and flexible.

TRAINING AIDS

Training must be based on an in-depth analysis of the sport to determine the movements required and the type of physical conditioning necessary to formulate a sound, beneficial conditioning program for optimum results. In stick fighting, the movements are centered on strikes and thrusts. Use of training aids must be based on exercises that simulate the movements of the art. Training aids do not have to be expensive, state-of-the-art, high technology gadgets. Training aids may be made from items readily available, and can normally be found around the yard, in the gym or in the martial arts school. The most useful and available device is a tree in the backyard. You can hang a *pabitin* (piece of stick or a used car tire) from a tree branch. For accuracy training, you can hang a tennis ball with a string passing through it from a tree branch. You can also use the tree trunk as a hitting pole. In order to have the "feel" of hitting flesh and also cushion the impact, you can put strips of discarded tire or used rubber slippers fastened around the tree trunk. Marking the exact target offers training in accuracy.

Most gyms and martial art schools have modern equipment that are very beneficial in training, such as a heavy bag or a "target or dummy tree." These training aids, however, may be too expensive for "backyard or garage" training. Use what you can to train well.

SUPPLEMENTARY EXERCISES

Aerobics—Running or any similar aerobic exercise should be a part of a physical conditioning routine. Running is an excellent form of endurance training for any athlete even if their moment of exertion in the arena lasts only a few seconds at a time. Other types of endurance training are stationary running, cycling, squat kicks or jumping rope. Swimming is also a good form of endurance training.

There are different kinds of running. To improve the oxygen-carbon dioxide exchange process, one must run at a slower pace but longer distance. To increase the amount of blood pumped by the heart, interval running is preferable. In this manner, you run fast for a certain distance to increase your heartbeat and then slow down until your heartbeat returns to normal. Repeat the process several times. This type of running improves the heart rate and overall cardiovascular conditioning.

"Do it right the first time, so you do not have to do it again."

Progressive Resistance Training—Weight training is highly recommended for strength development. Strength helps coordination and control. It increases speed and enhance stamina. Most of all it optimizes the explosiveness of the muscles. Explosive force makes the execution of skills easier. It also aids in balance, depth perception, and judgment of space and distance. Strength prevents injuries. In starting a weight-training regimen, use weight that allows you to do seven to eight repetitions without forcing yourself at the last repetition. When the weight gets too light (you can do 10 to 12 repetitions without forcing yourself), add about five pounds for upper body exercises and about ten pounds for lower body exercises. Repeat the process as your strength increases. Lift the weight as fast as you can without losing the right form. Proper breathing is very important. Go through the complete range of motion for all repetitions. There are an infinite number of weight training exercises. Select exercises that will work specifically for your sport. One of the best weight-training gadgets is the "Indian club." The Arnis stick itself can serve as an "Indian club" by securely attaching weight on the tip of the stick.

Free Hand Exercises—Two no-gadget exercises that are very effective in building upper body strength are push-ups and pull-ups. For lower body explosive power, jumping with both feet and bringing your knees to the chest level and then "bouncing like a ball" as fast as you can is very effective. Be creative when you do these exercises. Stretching exercises, such as yoga poses, are also very beneficial and a good way to promote relaxation.

CHAPTER 3

FUNDAMENTAL TRAINING

STANCE AND CENTER OF GRAVITY

There are two major classifications of stance, the knees-straight stance, and the knees-bent stance. Both stances may be the foundation of any technique, defensive or offensive. However, for maximum leverage, knees-straight stance is better utilized as a preparatory stance, and the knees-bent stance as a fighting stance or stance of execution.

There are three components governing the stance:

1. The stance must offer stability so proper traction can be achieved for fast and powerful techniques.

2. It must be comfortable so one can assume the posture without undue fatigue.

3. The stance must be flexible to allow excellent mobility.

The essence that holds these components together is the center of gravity. The center of gravity is the point where perfect equilibrium is situated. In Oriental philosophy, the center of gravity is the spot where the "center of consciousness resides." It is the point where power is stored and then projected and directed to a specific target. The center of gravity must be dynamic. As the stance or posture change, so does the center of gravity. In a forward movement, the center of gravity must move forward; in a backward movement, the center of gravity must move backward; and, in a sideward movement, the center of gravity must move sideward.

Stance and center of gravity cannot be separated. Stance is visible to the eye, while the center of gravity is the incorporeal state that exists without any material substance but holds all physical essence together.

To achieve stability, comfort and flexibility, the center of gravity must always fall within the stance. The common denominator in the stance's stability, comfort, and flexibility is the student's physiology and capability.

Characteristics of the Primary Fighting Stance

- Feet are spread hip width apart

- Weight is evenly distributed on both feet

- Knees are slightly bent and tensed outwards

The distance between the heel of the leading foot and the toes of the trailing foot must be equal to the length of your lower leg (knee to your foot),

- Toes of leading foot points directly forward

- Toes of trailing foot points about 15 to 30 degrees outwards

- Head, shoulders and hips must fall in a vertical line within the stance

FOOTWORK

Footwork is the process of moving, changing, shifting, progressing, ascending, descending, evolving, withdrawing, or advancing by stepping, sliding or jumping or a combination of these three actions to attack or to get out of the range of attack. The most important factor in footwork is maintaining balance at all times and keeping the center of gravity in the central point of the equilibrium. Body shifting is as much a part of footwork as the actual changing of one's stance.

Stepping Exercises from a Natural Stance

1. Move right foot forward to assume the right fighting stance.

2. Move right foot backward to assume the left cat stance.

3. Move right foot back to a natural stance.

1) Natural Stance

2) Stepping Right foot Forward To Fighting Stance

3) Stepping Right foot Backward to Left Cat Stance

4) Stepping Right Foot Forward to Natural Stance

1. Move left foot forward to assume a left fighting stance.

2. Move left foot backward to assume a right cat stance.

3. Move left foot back to a natural stance.

1) Natural Stance

2) Stepping Left Foot Forward to Left Fighting Stance

3) Stepping Left Foot Backward to Right Cat Stance

4) Stepping Left Foot Forward To Natural Stance

1. Move right foot backward to assume a left fighting stance.

2. Move left foot backward to assume a right cat stance.

3. Move left foot forward to assume left fighting stance

4. Move right foot forward to a natural stance.

1) Natural Stance

2) Stepping Right Foot Backward to Left Fighting Stance

3) Stepping Right foot Backward to Left Cat Stance

4) Stepping Left Foot forward to Left Fighting Stance

5) Step Right Foot Forward to Natural Stance

1. Move left foot backward to assume a right fighting stance.

2. Move right foot backward to assume a left cat stance.

3. Move right foot forward to assume a right fighting stance.

4. Move left foot forward to a natural stance.

1) Natural Stance

2) Stepping Left Foot Backward to Right Fighting Stance

3) Stepping Right Foot Backward to Left Cat Stance

4) Stepping Right Foreward to Right Fighting Stance

5) Step Left Foot Forward to Natural Stance

1. Move right foot to the right and turn 90 degrees to the left into a fighting stance.

2. Move left foot backward to assume a left cat stance.

3. Move left foot forward to assume a left fighting stance.

4. Move right foot forward to a natural stance as you turn 90 degrees to the right.

1) Natural Stance

2) Move Right Foot and Ready to Turn 90 Degree

3) Ready to Turn 90 Degree Left

4) Into Left Fighting Stance

5) Pull Left foot Back

6) To Left Cat Stance

7) Ready to Move Left foot Forward

8) Into Left Fighting Stance copy

9) Ready for Natural Stance

10) Back to Natural Stance

1. Move left foot to the left and turn 90 degrees to the right into a right fighting stance.

2. Move right foot backward to assume a right cat stance.

3. Move right foot forward to assume a right fighting stance.

4. Move left foot forward to a natural stance as you turn 90 degrees to the left.

1) Natural Stance

2) Move Left Foot and Ready to Turn 90 Degree

3) Ready to Turn 90 Degree Right

4) Into Right Fighting Stance

5) Pull Right Foot Back

6) To Right Cat Stance

7) Ready to Move Right Foot Forward

8) Into Right Fighting Stance

9) Ready for Natural Stance

10) Back to Natural Stance

Stepping/Sliding Exercises from a Natural Stance

1. Take a very long step forward with the right foot and then slide your left foot towards your right foot to assume a right fighting stance.

2. Move left foot back to its original position.

3. Move right foot back to assume the right cat stance.

4. Move right foot backwards to assume a natural stance.

1) Natural Stance

2) Ready for Right foot Long Step

3) Right Foot Long Step

4) Pulling Left Foot Forward

5) To Right Fighting Stance

6) Sliding Left Foot Back

7) Back to Right Long Step

8) Sliding Right Foot Back to Right Cat Stance

9) Pulling Right Foot Back to Natural Stance

1. Take a very long step forward with the left foot and then slide your right foot towards the left foot to assume a left fighting stance.

2. Move your right foot back to its original position.

3. Move your left foot back to assume a left cat stance.

4. Move your left foot to assume a natural stance.

1) Natural Stance

2) Ready for Left foot Long Step

3) Left Foot Long Step Forward

4) Pulling Right Foot Forward

5) To Left Fighting Stance

6) Sliding Right Foot Back

7) To Left Foot Long Step

8) Sliding Left Foot Back to Left Cat Stance

9) Pulling Left Foot Back to Natural Stance

1. Take a very long step to the right with the right foot and then slide your left foot towards the right foot to assume a left fighting stance while turning 90 degrees to the left.

2. Move your left foot back to its original position and move your right foot back to a natural stance while turning 90 degrees to the right.

1) Natural Stance

2) Long Step Right Foot

3) Slide your left foot towards the right foot

4) Turning 90 degrees [left] to fighting stance

5) Turning 90 degrees to the right sliding left foot back

6) Back to right long step position

7) Move right foot back to assume a natural stance

1. Take a very long step to the left with the left foot and slide your right foot towards the left foot to assume a right fighting stance and then turn 90 degrees to the right.

2. Move your right foot back to its original position and move left foot back to assume a natural stance while turning 90 degrees to the left

1) Natural Stance

2) Long Step Left Foot

3) Slide your Right foot towards the Left foot

4) Turning 90 degrees [right] to fighting stance

5) Turning 90 degrees to the left and sliding right foot back

6) Back to left long step position

7) Move left foot back to assume a natural stance

Jumping Exercises from a Natural Stance

1. Jump forward with both feet as far forward as you can and land in a right fighting stance.

2. Jump back to a natural stance.

1) From Natural Stance

2) Ready to Jump Forward

3) Jump Forward

4) Right Fighting Stance

5) Jump back

6) Jump Back to Natural Stance

1. Jump forward with both feet as far forward as you can and land in a left fighting stance.

2. Jump back to a natural stance.

1) From Natural Stance

2) Ready to Jump Forward

3) Jump Forward

4) To Left Fighting Stance

5) Jump back

6) Jump Back to Natural Stance

1. Jump backward with both feet as far back as you can and land in a right fighting stance.

2. Jump back forward to a natural stance.

1) From Natural Stance

2) Ready to Jump Backward

3) Jump Backward

4) To Right Fighting Stance

5) Jump Forward

6) Back to Natural Stance

1. Jump backward with both feet as far back as you can and land in a left fighting stance.

2. Jump back forward to a natural stance.

1) From Natural Stance

2) Ready to Jump Backward

3) Jump Backward

4) To Left Fighting Stance

5) Jump Forward

6) To Natural Stance

1. Jump to the left turning 90 degrees to the left and land in a left fighting stance.

2. Jump back to original position turning 90 degrees to the right and land in a natural stance.

1) Natural Stance

2) Ready 90 Degree jump

3) Jump Left

4) To Left Fighting Stance

5) Ready To Jump Back Right

7) Back to Natural Stance copy

1. Jump to the right turning 90 degrees to the right and land in a right fighting stance.

2. Jump back to original position turning 90 degrees to the left and land in a natural stance.

1) Natural Stance

2) Ready 90 Degree Jump

3) Jump Right

4) To Right Fighting Stance

5) Ready To Jump Left

7) Back to Natural Stance

1. Jump up turning 180 degrees to the left and land in a left fighting stance facing the opposite direction.

2. Jump up turning 180 degrees to the right and land in a natural stance.

1) From Natural Stance

2) Ready to jump 180

3) jump 180

4) Fighting stance

5) jump Back 180

6) jump back to Natural position

1. Jump up turning 180 degrees to the right and land in a right fighting stance facing the opposite direction.

2. Jump up turning 180 degrees to the left and land in a natural stance.

1) From Natural Stance

2) Ready to Jump

3) Jump

4) To Right Front Stance

5) Jump Back

6) Jump Back to Natural Stance

Alternating Stances from Fighting Stance to Cat Stance While Jumping from Kneeling Position

1. Kneel on both legs, crossing your feet behind you.

2. Jump up and assume the right fighting stance.

3. Jump back down to kneeling position.

1) From Kneeling Position

2) Ready to Jump

3) Jump Right

4) To Right Fighting Stance

5) Jump Back

6) Jump Back to Kneeling Position

1. Jump up and assume a left fighting stance.

2. Jump back down to a kneeling position.

1) From Kneeling Position

2) Ready to Jump

3) Jump Left

4) To Left Fighting Stance

5) Jump Back

6) Jump Back to Kneeling Position

1. Jump up and turn 180 degrees to the left and assume the left fighting stance.

2. Jump back down to kneeling position and turn 180 degrees to the right.

1) Kneeling Position

2) From your Toe's Ready to Turn

3) Ready to jump 180

4) jump 180

5)) Fighting stance

6) jump Back 180

7) Back to Kneeling Position

1. Jump up and turn 180 degrees to the right and assume right fighting stance.

2. Jump back down to kneeling position and turn 180 degrees to the left.

1) Kneeling Position

2) From your Toe's Ready to Turn

3) Ready to Jump

4) Jump 180

5) To Right Front Stance

6) Jump Back 180

7) Back to Kneeling Position

STICK GRIPS AND FULCRUMS

Before the development of Arnis de Mano, when swords were used, the butt of the handle extended only so much to secure the blade to the handle. The butt was not intended for any tactical purpose. In present day Arnis de Mano, the stick is held a few inches from the end to allow for disarming techniques, an innovation of the 20th century.

> "When faced with a challenge, some rise to the occasion while some rise above."

Some present day practitioners also insist that holding the stick about two inches from the end gives them more leverage, with the fulcrum on the stick and not on the wrist.

This is a postulation and is not supported by the laws of physics or the laws of motion.

- If you strike as if you are casting a fishing line, where you bend the wrist, then the wrist becomes the fulcrum.

A. Fishing Fulcrum 1

A. Fishing Fulcrum 2

- If you strike as you are hammering in a nail on a board with the wrist straight but the elbow bent, the elbow becomes the fulcrum.

B. Hammering Fulcurm 1

B. Hammering Fulcurm 2

- If you strike like a tennis player returning a smash with the whole arm straight, then the shoulder becomes the fulcrum.

C. Tennis Fulcrum 1

C. Tennis Fulcrum 2

- If you strike like a slugger hitting a fastball, then the hips become the fulcrum.

D. Slugger Fulcrum 1

D. Slugger Fulcrum 2

The power of the strike is not determined by whether you grip the stick at the very end or two inches from the end, but by the proper utilization of body mechanics.

There are two methods of holding the sticks, the old and the new. The old way was based on the use of the bladed weapon. The new way was based on the use of the stick or cane. The old way of holding the bladed weapon was grasping the handle almost all the way to the end of the handle. Bladed weapons normally have handles that fit the hands of the wielder exactly. This design of the Filipino bladed weapon was dictated by its use. To add weight and balance to the sword, some blades have extended handles.

Unlike European fencing where the competitors deliver stabs and thrusts using wrist movement, Filipino bladed art is mostly hacking and cutting utilizing elbow, shoulder, and hip movement.

In European fencing, the competitors use their sword to block the opponent's thrusts. In the Filipino fighting arts, the blade is not used to block the opponent's strikes, but to dispose of the opponent. Instead of blocking the blade, the Filipino warrior goes for the hand or the arm to render it useless and then deliver the coup de grace for the kill. The blade is regarded sacred and must not be desecrated by hitting another blade. The footwork of a Filipino warrior is just as important as the skill in wielding the blade. Evasion by bobbing, dodging or weaving takes precedence over blocking the strike.

When the Spaniards banned the practice of the fighting arts and the possession of the curved fighting blades, the use of the stick or cane was introduced. Instead of the one-strike, one-kill maneuvers, the art of wielding the stick was disguised in dance and theatrical performances.

"Linear strikes must be like a runaway locomotive destroying everything in its path. Circular strike must be like a tornado devastating everything that stands in its way."

Based on the techniques of the bladed weapon, the use of the stick took on a new direction. The stick was still held like a bladed weapon (almost to the end of the stick) and followed the cutting movement of the blade. Stickwork also copied the basics of European fencing's thrusts, strikes, and blocks.

Through the passage of time, the bladed weapon took on a different shape and design. From the curved fighting blade during the time of Rajah Lapu-lapu, it changed to the utilitarian straight edge blade that was allowed for food production. When Andres Bonifacio shouted his famous "Cry of Balintawak," he used a straight edge *itak, tabak, or gulok.*

When Spain gave up its claim of the Philippines to the United States in the Treaty of Paris, it was the straight edge *itak* that was the weapon of choice for the Filipino revolutionaries.

When Japan declared war against the United States, the Philippines were drawn into the World War Two. After the Americans surrendered, the Japanese occupied the Philippines. Guerilla warfare witnessed the resurgence of the straight edge blade and in some instances, the curved blade weapon, for a quick and silent kill. The straight edge *itak* was designed in such a way that the hand fits the handle almost to the very end.

After the war, carrying of bladed weapon was prohibited once more, this time by the civilian and police authorities. The mid twentieth century marked the revival of stick fighting. The use of the stick further evolved and the period marked the new golden age of the Filipino Fighting Art.

New masters of Arnis de Mano incorporated disarming and submission techniques. The way the stick was held changed. The stick is now held about two-inches from the end. The butt was used for disarming and for thrusting. The Filipino fighting art is now the premier 21st century international combative art.

Several elderly masters of Arnis de Mano, however, have a disdain for disarming techniques, and claim that if your stick can be disarmed, you are not good enough to be called an *arnisador*. The ancient disarming technique was to cut off the arm or to hit the hand so the opponent will automatically drop his weapon.

Whether you hold the stick at the very end or two inches from the end, the stick must be held tightly and securely with the thumb over the forefinger. Effectiveness of the techniques is not dependent on whether the stick is held at the very end or about two-inches from the end.

STICK STRIKING POSITIONS

Just as there are differences in gripping the stick, there are differences in wielding the stick. Handling the stick is determined by the type of play the *arnisador* favors. Offensive players position the stick in an offensive manner. Defensive players position the stick in a defensive manner. Whether you wield the stick offensively or defensively, you must always bear in mind the factors that determine the success of your strategy. The number one factor is how quick you can react between identification of the threat and response to the threat. The second factor is how effectively you can maximize your body mechanics in relation to the manner you wield the stick.

Stick Striking Positions

There are techniques where the stick is held in front of the body. There are techniques where the stick is rested on the shoulder. There are also techniques when the stick is held behind the shoulder and the ends of the stick are both held over and under the shoulder in an effort to confuse the opponent. Sometimes the stick is held on both ends but kept in front of the body. Sometimes the stick is held low and pointing to the ground.

A. Sticks are In Front of Body

B. Stick Rests on Shoulder

C. Stick Is Behind the Shoulder

D. Sticks are Over and Under shoulder

How the stick is wielded must be determined by the technique a player or practitioner employs. However, the position must not be so obvious that the opponent can gauge what to expect. Constant training and keen observation makes it possible for a perceptive student to anticipate an opponent's techniques by the way the stick is gripped, the way it is wielded, and the stance assumed.

"Do not compare yourself to others. There will always be one better or lesser than yourself. Enjoy your achievements and strive to improve always."

The stick must be held in a manner that may be considered defensive by some or offensive by others. This is because in Filipino martial arts the difference between offense and defense, to an observant student, is only a perception. With training and keen observation, it is possible to anticipate the opponent's actions and react or act pro-actively accordingly.

The regulation size of Arnis De Mano sticks was, originally, the length of the stick based on the practitioner's arm length from the tip of the middle finger to the armpit.

Generlly accepted other sticks:

- Junior size: 24-inches in length, 1–inch diameter
- Senior size: 28-inches in length, 1-inch diameter

Note: There are schools that allow 32-inch length sticks in training but these are not permitted in tournaments.

PATTERNS OF MOTIONS

Strikes have two particular patterns of motion—a line and a circle. In active form, they are referred to as linear and circular.

A straight line is the shortest distance between two points. Since it is the shortest distance, a linear strike is therefore the quickest strike. Due to the short distance the strike travels, it may not gain enough momentum to generate power. This is where body mechanics, stance, transfer of weight, manipulation of the center of gravity, direct application of force, and leverage all come into play. When all these variables are factored into the technique, the quickest strike can result in a very powerful strike. The linear pattern may go up and down in a vertical plane, side to side in a horizontal plane, or diagonally up and down.

By combining, connecting or intersecting straight lines, several patterns may be formed, such as a square, a triangle, a star or five-pointed shape, an asterisk or six-pointed shape, an octagon or eight-pointed shape or geometric symbols such as multiplication, addition or equals signs.

The linear strike results in the formation of four equidistant or quadrant strikes that are cross like in formation, resembling a multiplication sign or an addition sign.

The circular strike may be classified into an arc (a segment of a circle or a semi-circle), a spiral (circling again and again in different levels along a point), a complete circle where the strike starts and ends at the same point or a combination of all three to form a figure eight or a modified figure eight.

There are two forces that create the energy produced in the tornado- or twister-like circular pattern, the outward or centrifugal force and the inward or centripetal force.

A combination of the linear and circular strikes where the strikes touch each other, but are not intersecting each other, are called tangent strikes. When the straight line passes across or intersects with the circle, it is called a transverse strike.

The student must be taught never to stop striking until the threat is completely eliminated. Strikes may originate as a linear strike and evolve to a spiral pattern or start as a circular strike and develop into a linear strike or they may even be combined as a tangent strike or transverse strike.

Linear strikes must be like a runaway locomotive destroying everything in its path. Circular strike must be like a tornado devastating everything that stands in its way.

All maneuvers in stick fighting — quadrant, weaving, vertical, horizontal, arc, spiral, figure eight and circle strikes and other variations with different names — are evolutions of linear strike to circular strike or circular strike to linear strike or a combination of both.

Linear Strike

- **A – B** – The shortest distance from one point to another is a straight line.

- **X** Four quadrant strikes – Multiplication sign (natural reflex action)

- **+** Four equidistant strikes – Addition sign (acquired action)

- When you combine the multiplication and vertical or horizontal lines, you create the star (five-point strike) or asterisk (six-point strike)

- When you combine the multiplication and addition signs, you create the octagon (eight-point strike)

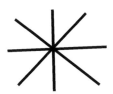

Circular Strike

- ∩ Arc – semi circle or segment of a circle

- O Circle – the strike starts and ends at the same point

- ∂ Spiral – the strike (circular motion) starts and ends on different planes

- ∞8 Figure eight – horizontal or vertical

- § Modified figure eight

Combination Linear and Circular Strikes

- ¢ Combination of arc and diagonal linear strike (transverse strike)

- ð Combination of spiral and diagonal linear strike (transverse strike)

- $ Modified figure eight and downward linear strike (transverse strike)

- Linear strike intersects with circular strike (transverse strike)

- Tangent strike – an arc or semi-circle and linear strikes, touching but not intersecting (the "small circle" strike is primarily used for deflection)

"The power of the strike is not determined by whether you grip the stick at the very end or two inches from the end, but by the proper utilization of body mechanics."

CHAPTER 4

DEFENSIVE ACTIONS

Defensive action is the strategy used to avoid being struck. This term is preferred over the most common term, "block," which carries a negative connotation. Literally, the term block means to stop the attack. It is a highly illogical method of defense because it suggests attempting to stop force with force. If you block using force against force, the greater force will prevail.

There are several methods to avoid being struck. Stepping back to get out of the range of the attack is the most natural reflex action. However, stepping back out of the range of the attack is devoid of logic since it also gets an individual out of range for an effective counter-attack. The better choice is evasion by stepping in, stepping to the side, or simple body-shifting which will take you to an effective counter-attack range, while preventing you from being hit. Two other ways of avoiding being struck are deflecting the strike or checking before the strike.

DEFLECTING

Deflecting the strike is an action taken after your opponent has delivered his blow. To deflect the strike does not mean attempting to stop the blow, but redirecting the motion of the blow away from you. This can be accomplished with a "small circle" strike or tangent strike. The action of the circular strike redirects the motion of the force of the attack. To better understand this concept, you need to think in mechanical terms. The rotational motion of the drive shaft

Deflecting 1   *Deflecting 2*

of an automobile converts into a forward or backward motion of the wheels through the axle by the gears.

When your opponent is already committed in his strike, you redirect the blow by a circular strike on your opponent's stick as you shift your body by stepping to the sides or inwards, changing your stance or by simple weight transfer.

Your strike must be aimed at the part of the stick between the tip and the middle. The part of the stick from the middle to the opponent's hand carries most of the weight of the strike and the attacker and is more difficult to deflect. Moreover, the opponent may change the direction of the attack by a simple twist of the wrist. With the tip of the opponent's stick out of range, you can convert the deflection into a counter-attack.

Body shifting, weight transfer or hip twisting is an important part of deflection. Since most initial strikes are linear strikes, the strike travels a shorter distance and is comparably faster than a circular strike. However, the deflection's circular motion generates energy that easily converts into an effective counter-strike.

CHECKING

Checking is a very effective and more assertive and progressive method of defense. The main purpose of checking is to "end the confrontation before it starts." It is a defensive action in the intuitive state and requires serious, intense training. An attack is not just the actual act of assault. It also means the aggressive intent to do harm. To have the ability to "sense" malicious intention takes a lot of perception and observation. You do not have to be a mind reader, but you must be able to discern the most subtle movements of the opponent. The look in an opponent's eyes and his or her breathing patterns are signs that must be considered.

Your opponent's stance and posture, how he wields his weapon and his distance from you are telltale signs of the techniques he can deliver. Look at your opponent as a whole without concentrating on any given point.

"Nurture strength of spirit and strength of body will follow."

Your stance and posture in relation to your opponent; the manner in which you wield your weapon compared to your opponent's; the distance from your opponent, and your level of training are some of the factors that must be considered in checking tactics.

Checking is a first strike tactic that is a defensive strike strategy to prevent the opponent from launching an attack. When the opponent "thinks" of attacking, you check the hand, shoulders or hips, depending on what you perceive will be the attack. Checking is not practical for contests and tournaments and may even be considered an illegal technique. However, for self-defense, it is a higher and more effective form of defensive action. Most, if not all targets of checking techniques, are delivered on parts of the body to prevent the opponent from being able to deliver a strike.

Checking 1

Checking 2

The most common targets of checking techniques are the wrists, just below the base of the thumb, in order to force the opponent to drop the stick, and breaking the opponent's clavicle so he will not be able to raise his arm.

The most common target of the tip of the stick is the armpit. An injury to the armpit causes weakness and chest pains, which affect breathing.

The most common target of the butt of the stick is the hollow area of the clavicle also known as the shoulder well. An injury to this area impedes the flow of blood to the brain and may result in going in and out of consciousness. It is possible to pierce the heart through the shoulder well by using a long knife.

Hitting the armpit or the shoulder well will prevent the opponent from raising the hand to strike.

EVADING

An integral component of defensive action is bobbing, weaving, dodging, or evasion. Basically all of these actions have the same meaning and share the goal of "not being in the place where the strike hits."

These actions may be achieved by sidestepping, changing of stance or simple weight transfer or hip twisting. Whatever action one takes, an important consideration is never to lose track of the opponent and his weapon. All these actions must be a part of both deflecting and checking strategies.

Evading 1

Evading 2

TRAPPING AND DISARMING

A natural consequence of evasion, deflecting and checking are trapping and disarming. Trapping is a strategy that allows you to capture the opponent's attacking limb in order to neutralize the threat. After trapping, you maneuver the opponent for the appropriate disarming technique.

There are systems that teach disarming techniques as initial tactics. For a more efficient disarming strategy, before the attempt to disarm or apply submission techniques, it is imperative you inflict pain and injury on the opponent to break his balance. The most effective manners of off-balancing your opponent are:

- Thrust to the eyes so the opponent cannot see;

- Thrust to the throat so the opponent cannot breath;

- Thrust to the groin so the opponent will bring his guard down; and

- Breaking the opponent's knee so the opponent cannot stand or breaking the shoulder or the arm so the opponent cannot wield a weapon.

Trapping 1

Trapping 2

Trapping 3

No matter what the weapon, joint-reversal (*pagsaliwa ng hugpungan*) is the basic maneuver in disarming techniques. There are two methods of joint reversal:

1. The arm turn (*pilipit ng braso*). Turning the thumb side of the wrist outwards from the vertical midline of the body.
2. The arm twist (*baliti ng braso*). Turning the thumb side of the wrist inwards to the vertical midline of the body.

There are disarming techniques that use the opposing scissor movement on the arms or even the stick itself. There are also techniques which utilize an attack on the elbow in a locking or breaking motion. Whatever disarming technique is used, it is always advisable to break the opponent's balance first by inflicting pain before the actual action of disarming.

Always defend yourself before the opponent attacks.

CHAPTER 5

STRIKING AND THRUSTING METHODS

STRIKING TARGETS

- Superior area (cephalic): Any part of the body from the waist to the head
- Inferior area (caudal): Any part of the body from the waist down to the feet
- Medial (inward): Any motion directed towards the vertical midline
- Lateral (outward): Any motion directed outwards from the vertical midline
- Proximal: Any extremity close to the trunk of the body
- Distal: Any extremity (arm, leg) that is farther away from the trunk (body core)
- Horizontal midline: Approximately at the waistline
- Vertical midline: The imaginary line separating the right and left sides of the body
- Anterior/ventral: The front part of the body
- Posterior/dorsal: The back part of the body

Right Side

Left Side

Superior Area (Cephalic)

Medial (Inward) - Any Motion Directed Towards the Vertical Midline

Proximal (Any Extremity Closer to the Trunk)

Horizontal Midline - Approximately the Waistline

Distal (Any Extremity Farther from the Trunk)

Inferior Area (Caudal) - Any Part from the Waist Down to the Feet

Lateral (Outward) Any Motion Directed Outwards the Vertical Midline

Vertical Midline

Posterior / Dorsal (Back Part of the Body)

Anterior / Ventral (Front Part of the Body)

Target Classifications

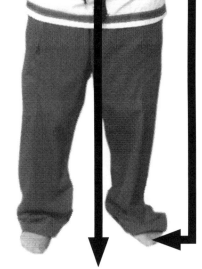

Superior Area – Above
Horizontal Midline

Killing Areas –
Head, Face, Neck, Torso,
Shoulders

Horizontal Midline

Disabling Areas – Hips
Thighs,
Lower Legs

Non-Lethal Areas –
Extremities: Upper and
Lower Arms, Hands and
Feet

Inferior Area – Below
Horizontal Midline

Vertical Midline

THE TWO UNIVERSAL STRIKES

In Arnis de Mano, there are two types of blows: the strike *(hablig)* and the thrust *(ulos)*. In English terminology, these terms may be used interchangeably. In Filipino terminology, these terms convey two different actions. A strike *(hablig)* is normally delivered in an angular cutting, slicing, slashing or snapping motion (like a whip). A thrust *(ulos, tusok, saksak)* is normally delivered in a straight forward, upward or downward stabbing, piercing motion.

With the different named styles and countless techniques of Arnis de Mano, there actually are only two classifications of strikes. They are the *hablig na palabas* (outward strike) and the *hablig na papasok* (inward strike). To better understand this concept, one has to think in tennis terms. In tennis there is the forehand (inward strike) and the backhand (outward strike). In more technical terms, a forehand strike is also called *medial strike* and the backhand strike is also called a *lateral strike*. As in tennis, the strikes are oriented from the perspective of the person delivering the strike, which is determined by the grip on the stick in relation to the direction of the strike.

"With the different named styles and countless techniques of Arnis de Mano, there actually are only two classifications of strikes: inward and outward or forehand and backhand."

The body is hypothetically divided vertically in the middle. This hypothetical division is called the vertical midline or the *centerline of the body*. Any strike directed towards the vertical midline is called *hablig na papasok* (inward strike, forehand strike or medial strike). Any strike directed away from the vertical midline is called *hablig na palabas* (outward strike, backhand strike or lateral strike). Strikes, whether offensive or defensive, fall under the category of forehand strike or backhand strike.

Put another way, if you are holding the weapon with your right hand and you strike in the direction of your left side, the strike is classified as an inward or forehand strike. When you are holding the weapon with your right hand and you strike in the direction of your right side, the strike is classified as an outward or backhand strike. In the same token, when you are holding the

Forehand - Front View

Forehand - Side View

Forehand 1 (front) Forehand 2 (front) Forehand 1 (side) Forehand 2 (side)

weapon in your left hand and you strike in the direction of your right side, the strike is classified as an inward or forehand strike. When you are holding the weapon with your left hand and you strike in the direction of your left side, the strike is classified as an outward or backhand strike.

For all intents and purposes, a downward strike to the crown of the head in the direction of the vertical midline or centerline of the body is classified as an inward or forehand strike.

Backhand - Front View

Backhand - Side View

Backhand 1 (front) Backhand 2 (front) Backhand 1 (side) Backhand 2 (side)

STRIKING AND THRUSTING METHODS | 75

A strike to the groin is classified as an inward or forehand strike when the palm is up. When the palm is down, the strike is classified as an outward or backhand strike.

No matter what maneuver one executes, whether it is the up and down vertical strikes, the side-to-side horizontal strikes or the circular or roundabout strikes, the strike originates as either a forehand or a backhand strike.

A forehand strike may be delivered with the leading hand or the trailing hand. Likewise, the backhand strike may be delivered with the leading hand or the trailing hand. Both strikes may be delivered from a regular stance (the leading hand is the same side as the leading foot) or the reverse stance (leading hand is the opposite side of the leading foot).

The most important factors in any strike, whether forehand or backhand, are form and technique. There was a time when a Filipino warrior depended solely on sheer brute force, not considering style or form important.

With the evolution of the art, body mechanics, leverage, and utilization of the center of gravity have elevated the strike to a higher and more powerful level. Proper style or form eliminates "wasted movements" and increases speed and energy.

There are three levels of target of both forehand and backhand strikes: upper, middle and lower. In the upper level, the most common strike is a strike to the head, the neck or the shoulder in a downward motion. There is a deceptive strike in this level, which is a strike to the head or the neck in an upward motion. In the middle level, the most common is to strike the arms, sides or hipbone in a sideward cutting motion. In the lower level, the most common is a strike to the knee in a downward motion. There is a deceptive strike in this level, which is an upward strike to the groin.

EXERCISES AND DRILLS

All basic exercises must be performed with two sticks. This is to instill in the student the need and importance of developing both the strong and the weak hand from the very onset of training. If only one stick is used, the student will favor one hand over the other and lose the fundamental nature of being able to fight with either hand or just the "weaker" hand in case the "strong" hand is incapacitated. This condition is called a "one-sided fighter," which can be a fatal flaw.

Note: The first set of exercises will be upper strikes. The second set of exercises will be middle strikes. The third set of exercises will be lower strikes

Step Left Forward Forehand and Reverse Right Forehand

- From natural stance, move left foot forward to the left oblique to assume a left fighting stance and then deliver a forehand strike with the leading (left) hand.

- Follow with a forehand strike with the reverse (right) hand.

- Move left foot back to natural stance.

1) Natural Stance   2) Step Left to Fighting Stance   3) Left Forehand Strike   4) Right Reverse Forehand Strike   5) Step Back Left To Natural Stance

Right Forehand and Left Forehand

- From natural stance, move the right foot forward to the right oblique to assume a right fighting stance then deliver a forehand strike with the leading (right) hand.

- Follow with a forehand strike with the reverse (left) hand.

- Move the right foot back to a natural stance.

1) Natural Stance

2) Step Right to Fighting Stance

3) Right Forehand Strike

4) Left Reverse Forehand Strike

5) Step Back Right to Natural Stance

Left Forehand and Reverse Right Forehand

- From a natural stance, move the right foot to the right and pivot on the left foot to face 90-degrees to the left and assume a left, fighting stance and then deliver a forehand strike with the leading (left) hand.

- Follow with a forehand strike with the reverse (right) hand.

- Move the right foot back to a natural stance, pivoting on your left foot to face 90-degrees to the right (original position).

1) Natural Stance

2) Step Right

3) Turn 90 Degree to the Left

4) To Left Fighting Stance

5) Ready for Left Forehand Strike

6) Left Forehand Strike

7) Ready for Reverse Right Forehand

8) Right Reverse Forehand Strike

9) Ready for Natural Stance

10) Back to Natural Stance

Right Forehand and Reverse Left Forehand

- From the natural stance, move the left foot to the left and pivot on the right foot to face 90-degrees to the right to assume a right fighting stance and then deliver a forehand strike with the leading (right) hand.

- Follow with a forehand strike with the reverse (left) hand.

- Move the left foot to a natural stance pivoting on the right foot to face 90-degrees to the left (original position).

1) Natural Stance   2) Step Left   3) Turn 90 Degree to the Right   4) To Right Fighting Stance   5) Ready for Right Forehand

6) Right Forehand Strike   7) Ready for Reverse Left Forehand   8) Left Reverse Forehand Strike   9) Ready for Natural Stance   10) Back to Natural Stance

Right Step Back Left Forehand and Reverse Right Forehand

- From a natural stance, move the right foot back to the right oblique to assume a left fighting stance and then deliver a forehand strike with the leading (left) hand.

- Follow with a forehand strike with the reverse (right) hand.

- Move the right foot forward to assume a natural stance.

1) Natural Stance   2) Right Step Back to Fighting Stance   3) Left Forehand Strike   4) Right Reverse Forehand Strike   5) Step Right Forward to Natural Stance

Left Step Back Right Forehand and Reverse Left Forehand

- From a natural stance move the left foot back to the left oblique to assume a right fighting stance and then deliver a forehand strike with the leading (right) hand.

- Follow with a forehand strike with the reverse (left) hand.

- Move the left foot forward to assume a natural stance.

1) Natural Stance 2) Left Step Back to Fighting Stance 3) Right Forehand Strike 4) Left Reverse Forehand Strike 5) Step Left Forward to Natural Stance

PROGRESSION OF TRAINING

1. Move the foot to assume the stance and then deliver the first strike bringing the center of gravity down and exhaling through the mouth. Go back to original position

2. Move the foot to assume the stance as you deliver the first strike, bringing the opponent's center of gravity down. Hold your breath and then deliver the second strike as you exhale through the mouth and return to original position

3. Move the foot to assume the stance as you deliver the strikes in quick succession at the same time bringing the center of gravity down and exhaling through the mouth. Go back to original position.

4. Move the foot to assume the stance as you deliver strikes in quick succession as you exhale (*bun-yaw*) at the same time to bring down your opponent's center of gravity. Move to the stance and use strikes to bring down the center of gravity while exhaling (*bun-yaw*). All this must end at the same time. Go back to the original position.

BASIC THRUSTS

In the Filipino martial arts, a thrust (*ulos*) is different from a strike (*hablig*). While *hablig* is an angular, cutting, slicing, slashing or hacking maneuver, *ulos* is a forward stabbing, piercing, penetrating tactic. *Ulos* (sometimes also known as *saksak* or *tusok*) is delivered using the tip of the knife, the end of the stick or the butt of the stick.

Where the knife is concerned, whether it is used for stabbing or for slashing, the pattern it follows is the direction of the multiplication sign or X pattern. Originally used exclusively in close range knife fighting, the *ulos* became part of Arnis de Mano's *espada y daga* (sword and dagger) system. In the *doble baston* (double sticks) system, the tip and the butt are used as a knife.

> "No matter how many techniques or angles of strikes a school adopts, it can be simplified back to the four basic quadrant strikes and a forward thrust."

There are two directions of *ulos*, overhand *(pabulusok)* and underhand *(paahon)*. Overhand is executed normally in a downward motion with the hand raised above the elbow or the arm raised over the shoulder like a baseball pitcher throwing a fastball. Underhand is executed normally in an upward motion with the hand below the level of the elbow or the arm below the level of the shoulder similar to a softball pitch.

Any part of the body that is hit with a knife or the tip or the butt of the stick will cause injury; however, since the Filipino martial art's principle is "one-strike, one-kill," there are specific targets that help achieve this goal.

The two main targets of an overhand knife thrust are the carotid arteries on the sides of the neck. Cutting or severing the carotid artery causes severe bleeding, depleting blood to the brain and other parts of the body that cause a fatal result.

The two main targets of an underhand knife thrust are the heart and the liver. Injury to the heart disrupts the efficient pumping action of the organ. When the heart is damaged, blood supply is disrupted which normally has a fatal result. Damage to the liver may cause both external and internal bleeding, which likewise may be fatal.

Injury caused by the tip or the butt of the stick may not cause bleeding, but may cause severe trauma that is just as deadly and fatal as an injury caused by a knife.

The underhand thrust to the heart was the thrust of choice when live blades were used. With the advent of the use of sticks, several variations were adopted. Thrusts to the eyes and other parts of the body were added to the repertoire of Arnis blows. Some stick-fighting schools employ as many thrusts as they do strikes in their training.

A thrust, particularly the underhand thrust is a very deceptive maneuver. In tournaments, the thrust is rarely used or allowed despite its effectiveness and speed of delivery. In defensive situations, the thrust stands out as a decisive blow that is quick to employ and not easy to block or defend against. The downside of the thrust is it is practical for close-range and middle-range fighting, but impractical for long-range fighting unless using a sword or a long stick.

Note: The basic pattern of thrust motions is the multiplication sign or the X pattern.

ANGLES AND STRATEGIES

There are two main actions that determine the direction of the strikes or thrusts and techniques of Arnis de Mano. The first are the "natural reflex actions" and the second are the "acquired structured actions."

The "natural reflex actions" are actions that the body "wants" to perform without conscious effort due to the fundamental muscle formation and development. The "acquired structured actions" are actions that are learned and taken with conscious effort and require muscle "repositioning."

Angles and Strategies

To better understand this concept, stand up straight and let your hands fall naturally to the side of the body. The palms will automatically face inside. When you bring them up to chest level, the palms will still face inside towards each other without any conscious effort on your part. These are "neutral" positions caused by the natural formation of the muscles.

When you hold your weapon at chest level, your arm "wants" to strike downward in either a right or left oblique direction. When you hold your weapon at knee level, your arm "wants" to strike upward either in the right or left oblique direction. These movements are the most natural actions due to the "neutral" muscle position.

Hands Down   Hands Up   Stick Hands Up   Sticks Down

The design of the blades used by the early Filipino warriors were configured for cutting, hacking, slicing and slashing. This blade characteristic suggests that in the early development of Arnis de Mano, fighters relied on "natural reflex actions," based on the four intrinsic angles or directions; the right oblique downward direction; the left oblique downward direction; the right oblique upward direction; and the left oblique upward direction.

> "Strive to be in good terms with all persons without surrendering your convictions, and principles."

These motions, form an X-pattern or a multiplication sign, are the most natural movements when you hold a sword to cut or a stick to strike or a knife to stab or slash.

NATURAL REFLEX ACTION ANGLES

Four quadrant or angles of directions (multiplication sign)

Left oblique downward   Right oblique downward

Left oblique upward   Right oblique upward

These four angles of directions are called the four quadrant or multiplication directions (strikes/thrusts).

Arnis de Mano's term for these four directions or four 90-degrees angles of strikes and thrusts is *kruzada* (**X** movement). *Kruzada* is the Spanish word for cross, whether it is the **X** (multiplication) sign or the **+** (addition) sign (or sign of the Christian faith). There is no clear distinction as to the difference, except in the context that the term is used. All techniques in Filipino stick fighting that resemble the "cross" are simply referred to as Kruzada.

For a better understanding of the evolution of *kruzada*, it is necessary to be familiar with the linear strikes involved in the system. There are three patterns of motion in *kruzada*—the diagonal up and down strikes (*tagang pahiwid or tirada*), the vertical up and down strikes (*tagang patayo*), and the horizontal side-to-side strikes (*tagang pahiga*).

The diagonal up and down strikes are known as the "natural angle strikes" and are determined by the "neutral position" of the muscles of the arm, which resulted in the design and configuration of the Filipino fighting blade (made for cutting and hacking).

The vertical up and down and the horizontal side-to-side strikes are referred to as "acquired angle strikes," because "repositioning" of the arm muscles are necessary to deliver these strikes.

> "In life's struggles, being second best may mean being dead."

The diagonal up and down strikes are the most basic *kruzada* strike, and, in fact sometimes considered the true *kruzada* strike.

With the influence of the theatrical forms of swordplay popularized by the *moro-moro* stage plays, the *kruzada* has been expanded to the asterisk (six-pointed strikes) and later to the octagon (eight-pointed strikes). The eight-pointed system was adopted as the basis of most stick-fighting styles or schools. However, there are schools that retained the original diagonal up and down maneuver as their *kruzada* system.

When the live blade was replaced with sticks, training in the fighting arts was concealed in dance movements. Straight up and down and side-to-side motions were developed to allow the practitioner more flexibility. This "acquired structured actions," which forms an addition or plus sign (+) were based on the bearings of the map.

When you look at a map there are four main directions. Up is north, down is south, right is east, and left is west. Each direction is 90-degrees from each other, which forms a cross or an addition, sign (in arithmetic terms).

LEARNED (ACQUIRED) ACTION ANGLES

Map angles (90 degrees of each other)

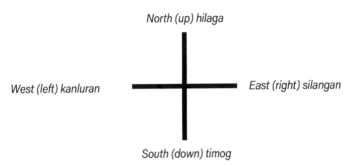

Superimposing the addition (+) with the multiplication (×) sign reduces the angle each direction forms to 45-degrees but increases the directions or angles to eight points (octagon):North, Northeast, East, Southeast, South, Southwest, West and Northwest.

Octagon (eight points): Combination of the multiplication and addition directions.

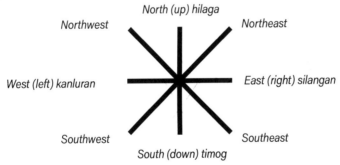

The octagon (eight point) strike was adopted as the standard by most stick fighting schools. When you replace the long blade with a short blade, like a dagger, the action the hand "wants" to go is into a thrust (*ulos, tusok or saksak*) directly forward (zero angle), either in an overhand or an underhand motion.

In the early stages of the art, there were the four basic quadrant strikes and a forward thrust. With the passage of time, some schools of Arnis de Mano expanded the strikes to the eight points (octagon) strike and the thrust to four separate variants: a pierce to the heart, a pierce to the liver and a poke to each eye (originally cutting the carotid artery on the sides of the neck). The eight strikes and the four thrusts became the basis of most of Arnis de Mano's 12 techniques of attack.

Other schools adopted eight angles of strikes and a single center thrust. However, no matter how many techniques or angles of strikes a school adopts, it can be re-simplified back to the four basic quadrant strikes and a forward thrust.

Note: The X-pattern and the forward thrust were the original directions of attack in the Filipino martial arts. Strikes with a stick or cut and a slash from a long or short knife follow the same pattern or direction.

The average fastball of a professional ball player is 90 feet per second going parallel to the ground. When you strike downward, the force of gravity must be factored. Studies have shown that due to the "neutral position of the muscles, the downward diagonal strike is the fastest and most powerful strike.

PART 2:

PRINCIPLES OF CLASSICAL MANEUVERS

The main classical maneuvers (or systems as some schools call them) evolved from the traditional techniques. Presented here are classical maneuvers that are common in most schools or styles of Arnis de Mano. There are other maneuvers that are variations and modifications of these main classical maneuvers, but may be called differently. Some schools may call the same maneuver one name when executed from a regular stance and another name when executed from a reverse stance. Some schools may call a maneuver differently when executed with the left hand first than when done with the right hand first. However, whatever the name, flexibility, and adaptability of Filipino stick fighting is evident with these classical maneuvers.

Each technique may be delivered individually, against a specific target or the classical maneuver may be used in a continuous motion against multiple opponents or to inflict multiple strikes against a single opponent. Whether it is against a single or multiple opponents, each technique has the potential to be fatal. The beauty of Arnis de Mano cannot be fully appreciated until one witnesses these classical maneuvers performed with double sticks. Unfortunately, with emphasis on "sports arnis," the use of single stick for a quick scoring technique is now more and more practiced at the expense of the double sticks. The glory of being called a tournament "winner" or "medalist" has taken precedence over appreciation of the beauty of the art. These classical maneuvers must not be viewed as different and separate principles, but rather as steps to a successful Filipino martial arts education.

CHAPTER 6

THE TWO BASIC STRIKES

Different schools or systems refer to strikes with various names. Some schools associate the name of the strike with the target. With these schools, a strike to the head may also be called a "right hand strike to the left side of the head." Some schools assign a number to a specific target. This is the common practice of most Arnis de Mano schools or styles. A strike to the left side of the head is called a "number one strike."

> "The most important factors in any strike, whether forehand or backhand, are form and technique."

When you ask different practitioners how many basic strikes they have in their school, it is not surprising to get different answers. There are schools that claim they have four basic strikes, two strikes to the opponent's left side and two strikes to the opponent's right side. By adding a strike to the top of the head, the five basic strikes school was born. Feeling a "need" to expand, other schools added one more strike to each side of the body. Influenced by the straight thrusts of European foil fencing, thrusting techniques to each eye, to the left, center and right chest were added. Whether it was to be different or they really felt the need, some schools added so many strikes and so many thrusts that the 12 basic strikes school developed and is now the most common. In order to confuse the opponent, some schools rotate the sequence of the strikes by not following the set routine of the original 12 strikes. Some schools have added more techniques and maneuvers in an attempt to make their school stand out.

However, are these additions considered basic strikes? When broken down, there are really only two basic strikes: the forehand strike and the backhand strike. This book was written to explain this in detail.

CONFUSING STRIKE NUMBERING

The head is the primary target. Number one is generally aimed at the left side of the head, number two is the right side, and the top of the head or the crown, which understandably must be the primary target, is assigned to number seven. This "strange" numbering can best be explained in the section titled, "Evolution of Strikes."

The number one strike is normally aimed at the left side of the head (since a greater number of *arnisadors* lead with the right hand) and the number two strike is to the right side of the head. The left side from the shoulder to the waist is number three, while the right side from the shoulder to the waist is number four. The lower left side (from the waist to the foot) is assigned number 5; number 6 is assigned to the lower right side (from the waist to the foot). Number seven, as stated earlier, is the top of the head. Targets of thrusts are also assigned numbers. The left eye is number eight and the right eye is number nine. Number 10 refers to a thrust to the left chest, while number 11 is a thrust to the right chest. A straight thrust to the middle of the chest is number 12. There really is no set basis for this numbering system, but the above is the most common practice.

"It takes the strength and courage of a warrior to take a step backwards."

To make things more confusing the arrangements of the strikes are based on different maneuvers. Some schools base their "basic strikes" on the *abaniko* (fanning strike). Others base it on the sinawali, while some base it on kruzada or the *redonda* (circular strike). There is nothing wrong with this approach because this is how one school differentiates their "style" from the other "styles." However, this is where the problem lies.

When you ask a practitioner of a particular style to demonstrate their basic strikes, they will normally say this is "number one strike" and perform a strike to the left side of the head. There may be a school that performs the same strike without the number identifier. There are styles that use the target as the name of the strikes. Instead of saying number one strike, they say strike to the left side of the head and so on. Then there are schools who will execute an *abaniko* (left and right strikes to the head) as their first "basic" strike.

To differentiate one style from another, some schools rotate the number of strikes and thrusts. However, if the "master" of the style is left-handed and leads with the left hand the whole number system is reversed. If the "master" is right-handed, his number one strike is a strike to the left side of the head. If the "master" is left-handed, and leads with his left hand, his number one strike is the right side of the head. This reversal of the numbering system can vary.

To avoid this confusion Arnis de Mano must be taught according to the guidelines of Filipino martial arts education. There must be a universally accepted terminology. Techniques must be broken down into the minutest elements. Scientific principles must govern the pattern of motion and the application of force. The two basic strikes must be referred to using standard terminology as simple as: forehand and backhand.

"Arnis de Mano must be taught according to the guidelines of Filipino martial arts education. There must be a universally accepted terminology. Techniques must be broken down into the minutest elements. Scientific principles must govern the pattern of motion and the application of force."

STRIKES IN FMA EDUCATION

The authors' approach to Arnis de Mano is based on the guidelines and princuiples of Filipino martial arts education. Filipino martial art education embraces the concept of the "principle of opposites," namely, the forehand and backhand strikes, linear and circular motions, and explains the strikes as such. Based on the logical development and relationships of the techniques and maneuvers, martial arts education may be taught in the most understandable manner.

Arnis de Mano contains two types of blows, the strike *(hablig or hampas)* and the thrust *(ulos, tusok, or saksak)*. A strike *(hablig or hampas)* is normally delivered in an angular cutting, slicing, slashing or snapping motion (like a whip).

A thrust *(ulos, tusok, saksak)* is normally delivered in a straight forward, upward or a downward stabbing, piercing penetrating motion.

To reiterate, inspite of the different named styles and countless techniques of Arnis de Mano, there are only two classifications of strikes: the *hablig na palabas* (outward strike) and the *hablig na papasok* (inward strike).

THE DIVIDED BODY

For a clearer understanding, the body is hypothetically divided vertically in the middle. This hypothetical division is called the *vertical midline* or the *centerline* of the body. Any strike directed towards the vertical midline (right to left or left to right) is called *hablig na papasok* (inward strike, forehand strike or medial strike). Any strike directed away from the vertical midline (right-to-right or left-to-left) is called *hablig na palabas* (outward strike, backhand strike or lateral strike). Strikes, whether offensive or defensive, fall under the category of forehand strike or backhand strike.

> "Some schools have added more techniques and maneuvers in an attempt to make their school stand out."

In simple interpretation, if you are holding the weapon with your right hand and you strike in the direction of your left side, the strike is classified as an inward or forehand strike. When you are holding the weapon with your right hand and you strike in the direction of your right side, the strike is classified as an outward or backhand strike. Conversely, when you are holding the weapon with your left hand and you strike in the direction of your right side, the strike is classified as an inward or forehand strike. When you are holding the weapon with your left hand and you strike in the direction of your left side, the strike is classified as an outward or backhand strike.

For all intents and purposes a downward strike to the crown of the head in the direction of the vertical midline or centerline of the body is classified as an inward or forehand strike. A strike to the groin is classified as an inward or a forehand strike when the palm is up. When the palm is down, the strike is

Forehand

classified as an outward or backhand strike. No matter what maneuver one executes, whether it is the up and down vertical strikes, the side-to-side horizontal strikes or the circular or roundabout strikes, the strike originates as either a forehand or a backhand strike.

A forehand strike may be delivered with the leading hand or the trailing hand. Likewise, the backhand strike may be delivered with the leading hand or the trailing hand. Both strikes may be delivered from a regular stance (leading hand is the same side as the leading foot) or the reverse stance (leading hand is the opposite side of the leading foot). The rule of the forehand and the backhand holds infinitely true, whether one is left-handed or right-handed.

Backhand

What's more, all basic exercises must be performed with two sticks to instill in the student the need and importance of developing both the strong and the weak hand from the very onset of training. If only one stick is used, the student will favor one hand over the other and lose the fundamental nature of being able to fight with either hand, or just the "weaker" hand in case the "strong" hand is incapacitated. This condition is called a "one-sided fighter," which may be a fatal flaw. The most important factors in any strike, whether forehand or backhand, are form and technique.

STRIKING LEVELS, POWER AND DELIVERY

There are three levels of target for both forehand and backhand strikes. They are upper, middle and lower.

Upper Level — The most common strike is a strike to the head, the neck or the shoulder in a downward motion. There is a deceptive strike in this level, which is a strike to the head or the neck in an upward motion.

Upper Level 1

Upper Level 2

Middle Level — The most common is strike is to the arms, sides or hipbone in a sideward cutting motion.

Middle Level 1

Middle Level 2

Lower Level 1   Lower Level 2

Lower Level — the most common is a strike to the knee in a downward motion. There is also a deceptive strike at this level, which is an upward strike to the groin.

The power of strikes and thrusts in Arnis de Mano is determined by three factors:

1. The backswing or windup;

2. The effective use of body mechanics including stance, use of leverage, weight transfer and distribution, hip rotation and the natural use of leveraging ability during the forward travel of the stick, and, finally, control and manipulation of the center of gravity (also referred to as transfer of motion);

3. The follow-through.

"All basic exercises must be performed with two sticks to instill in the student the need and importance of developing both the strong and the weak hand from the very onset of training."

These three components are inseparable parts of one motion. Remember the whole is the sum of all the parts.

Backswing is sometimes called wind-up or winding of the shoulders and hips. The opposite action or unwinding, also referred to as the transfer of motion from the stick to the target, and the follow-through determines the acceleration, which creates the power generated by the strike.

| Windup | Transfer of motion | Follow through |

Everybody's strike is the same. This is true, due to the structural use of the body, specifically the use of the arm does not change because it cannot. If it did, we will be witnessing a new evolutionary stage in human development. However, this does not mean that everyone's strikes have the same efficiency. Remember, not everybody is the same physiologically and psychologically. Find your best power source, whether it is a rotary movement, linear movement or angular movement to accelerate your strike in terms of speed and contact value. If acceleration is not correct, accuracy and power are lost. However, do not sacrifice accuracy for speed and power. Remember, a direct hit even by a .22 caliber is better than a near-hit of a .50 caliber.

Strikes may be delivered three ways:

1. With the flick of the wrist;
2. With the bending of the elbow;
3. With the swing of the arm as a unit.

"Filipino martial art education embraces the concept of the "principle of opposites," namely, the forehand and backhand strikes, linear and circular motions."

Your distance to your target is the determining factor on how you deliver the strike. There are teachers who say you have to keep your wrist fixed when striking. There are also teachers who say you have to keep your wrist flexible. In a strike where the wrist is the fulcrum, you need to keep the wrist flexible. When the elbow is the fulcrum, the wrist must be fixed. When you extend the arm as a unit with the shoulder as the fulcrum, the elbow and the wrist must be locked as the arm flexes laterally around you. In whatever strike you deliver, maximum efficiency may be attained ONLY by utilizing the principle of MIBOME.

A powerful forehand strike uses the arm in much the same way as an overhand fastball is thrown. A powerful backhand strike requires effective use of the opposite muscles utilized in the forehand strike at the point of contact with the target. The two basic strikes evolved into basic maneuvers, such as the *sinawali*, the *redonda*, the *kruzada*, and others. These basic maneuvers became the foundation of the different schools and styles.

CHAPTER 7

THE SIX CLASSICAL MANEUVERS

The following six striking maneuvers are common to all styles and schools of Arnis de Mano. In Filipino martial arts education, these maneuvers are called basic strikes of forehand and backhand. These each go by a specific name designation and while they all fall into forehand or backhand categories, their method of execution distinguishes them from one another.

FANNING (ABANIKO) MANEUVERS

This classical maneuver known as *abaniko* (fanning strike) is the most basic of all Arnis de Mano maneuvers. It is the very essence of the fundamental strikes—the forehand and the backhand strikes. Likewise, it also incorporates the attributes of the patterns of motion, linear and circular.

Basic strikes are distinguished by the position of the wrist. On the backhand strike, the wrist is turned with the palm facing down in a right-to-right or left-to-left direction. On the forehand strike, the wrist is turned with the palm facing up on a right-to-left or left-to-right direction. Both strikes may be delivered in a linear pattern or circular pattern.

By executing the side-to-side strikes in a circular motion, fanning strikes (Abaniko or pamaypay) were developed, evolving into three different maneuvers called the *abaniko* (fan), *corto* (short), the *medya* (middle) and the *largo* (long) techniques.

The *corto* (short), also sometimes called *panampal* (slapping), technique is characterized by the flicking of the wrist when changing the direction of the strike. In this strike, the wrist is the fulcrum. If you analyze the maneuver closely, you will see that these are actually two techniques in one motion. It may start as a forehand strike that will continue and end as a backhand strike. Alternatively, it may start as a backhand strike that will continue and end as a forehand strike.

"The characteristics of this blade design suggests that early on in the development of Arnis de Mano, fighters relied on "natural reflex actions," based on the four intrinsic angles or directions."

The most basic evolution of the circular pattern of motion is the *abaniko* or fanning strikes. From this simple maneuver, other more complex maneuvers such as the figure eight (*pigurang otso* the *redonda*, and other circular strikes came about.

The middle (*medya*) is characterized by the bending of the elbow as the fulcrum, with the strike going in a semi-circle direction from one side to the other. The position of the arm and the wrist changes with the direction of the strike.

The long (*largo*) is characterized by the swing of the whole arm with the shoulder as the fulcrum and the strike going in a semi-circle from one side to the other. The position of the arm and wrist change position with the change of the direction of the strike.

The next evolution of the circular strikes is the figure eight (*pigurang otso*). When you execute this maneuver, start slow and do it alternating the right and left hands. Then, do both hands at the same time. Do the complete range of motion as you increase striking speed. Then, do the maneuver as fast as you can while going backward, forward, sideward in a clockwise direction, and sideward in a counter-clockwise direction. Always visualize striking multiple opponents with each opponent being disposed of with each strike.

After you understand the underlying principles of the linear and circular strikes, you can start your training in the progressive stage.

In the short *abaniko* (*corto*), the wrist is the fulcrum.

Regular Stance

Reverse Stance

The middle (*medya*) is characterized by the bending of the elbow as the fulcrum, with the strike going in a semi-circle direction from one side to the other. The position of the arm and the wrist changes with the direction of the strike. The elbow is the fulcrum.

Forehand (Right to Left Strike)

Backhand (Left to right Strike)

The long (*largo*) is characterized by the swing of the whole arm with the shoulder and the whole body, acting in unison as the fulcrum with the strike going in a semi-circle from one side to the other. The position of the arm and the wrist change position with the change of the direction of the strike. In the *largo abaniko*, the elbow, shoulder and whole body are the fulcrum in unison.

Forehand (Right to Left Strike)

Backhand (Left to right Strike)

SIDE-TO-SIDE (BANDA Y BANDA) MANEUVERS

Also called *banda y banda*, side-to-side strikes are forehand or backhand linear strikes that are distinguished by the position of the wrist. On the backhand strike, the wrist is turned with the palm facing down in a right-to-right or left-to-left direction. On the forehand strike, the wrist is turned with the palm facing up in a right-to-left or a left-to-right direction. In the photos below we demonstrate the side-to-side strikes using a live blade, so the palm must always turn so the sharp edge cuts.

Forehand – Palm Up – Right to left

Backhand - Palm Down - Left to Right

CROSS (KRUZADA) MANEUVERS

Kruzada (*crossada*) is the Spanish word for cross, whether it is the **X** (multiplication) sign or the **+** (addition) sign. There is no clear distinction as to the difference except in how the term is used. Hence, all techniques in Filipino stick fighting that resemble the "cross" or crossed lines are simply referred to as *kruzada*.

The diagonal up and down strikes or the **X** (multiplication sign) are the most basic *kruzada* strike, and sometimes considered the "true *kruzada*" strike.

Broken down to its smallest component, the *kruzada* is made up of two basic strikes—the forehand strike and the backhand strike.

For a better understanding of the evolution of the *kruzada*, it is necessary to become familiar with the linear strikes involved in the maneuver. There are two patterns of linear motion in the *kruzada*: the diagonal up and down strikes.

The diagonal up and down strikes are known as the "natural angle strikes" determined by the "neutral position" of the muscles of the arm, which resulted in the design and configuration of the Filipino fighting blade (made for cutting and hacking).

The "natural reflex actions" are actions the body "wants" to perform without conscious effort due to its muscle formation and development. The "acquired structured actions," on the other hand, are actions that are learned and need conscious effort for muscle "repositioning."

To better understand this concept, stand up straight and let your hands fall naturally to the side of the body. The palms will automatically face inside. When you bring them up to chest level, the palms will still face inside towards each other without any conscious effort on your part. These are "neutral" positions caused by the natural formation of the muscles.

The palms facing each other is the "neutral" muscle position and the most natural action.

When you hold your weapon at chest level, your arm "wants" to strike downward either in a right oblique or a left oblique direction. When you hold your weapon at knee level, your arm "wants" to strike upward either in

a right oblique or left oblique direction. These movements are the most natural actions due to their "neutral" muscle position.

The design of the blades used by the early Filipino warriors were configured for cutting, hacking, slicing, and slashing. The characteristics of this blade design suggests that early on in the development of Arnis de Mano, fighters relied on "natural reflex actions," based on the four intrinsic angles or directions, as follows in the graphic:

Natural reflex action angles
Four directions (multiplication sign)

Left Oblique Downward Strike   Right Oblique Downward Strike

Left Oblique Upward Strike   Right Oblique Upward Strike

These motions, forming an X pattern or multiplication sign, are the most natural movements when one holds a sword to cut, a stick to strike or a knife to stab or slash.

In Filipino martial arts education, these four angles of directions are called the "four quadrant" or "multiplication direction" strikes/thrusts. As noted above, Arnis de Mano's term for these four directions or four 90-degrees angles of strikes/thrusts is *kruzada* (X movement).

The addition sign (+), composed of the vertical up-and-down and the horizontal side-to-side strikes, is referred to as "acquired angle strikes," because a "repositioning" of the arm muscles is necessary to deliver these strikes.

With the change in the design of the weapon, straight up-and-down (*rompida*) and side-to-side (*banda y banda*) motions were developed to allow practitioners more flexibility in techniques. These "acquired structured actions," which forms a plus sign (+) were based on the bearings of the map.

When you look at a map, there are four main directions: up is North, down is South, right is East, and left is West. This is why you say "up north, down south, back east and out west." Each direction is 90 degrees from the next, which forms a plus or the addition sign.

Learned (acquired) action angles addition sign
Map angles (90 degrees of each other)

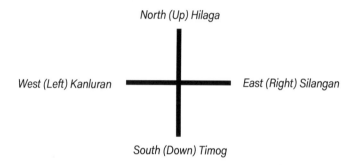

With the influence of the theatrical forms of swordplay popularized by the *mo-ro-moro*, the *kruzada* evolved to the asterisk and octagon strikes by adding the vertical up and down and the horizontal side-to-side strikes. The eight-pointed system was adopted as the basis of most stick-fighting styles or schools.

Superimposing the addition sign (+) with the multiplication sign (×), reduces the angle each direction forms to 45 degrees but increases the directions or angles to eight points of the compass.

The octagon – merging the natural reflex angle actions and the acquired angle actions

Octagon (eight points)

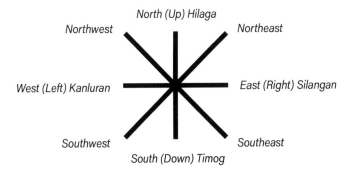

The octagon (eight points) strike has been adopted as the standard by most stick fighting schools. However, there are schools that have retained the original diagonal up and down maneuvers and refer to it as the "Four Basic Strikes *Kruzada* System." Moreover, there are schools that maintained the direction of the four basic *kruzada* strikes but added other strikes and thrusts in each direction, such as the *Kuatro Puntas Kruzada* system.

ORIGINAL KRUZADA

Using a bladed weapon

Natural angle strikes
(diagonal up and down
forehand-backhand
strikes)

Forehand inward downward strike

Backhand outward upward strike

Backhand outward downward

Forehand inward upward strike

KRUZADA

Using an Impact Weapon (Reverse Stance)

WEAVING (SINAWALI) MANEUVERS

Sinawali means weaving an intricate process of interlacing strands of bamboo or nipa into wall patterns or thread to make into cloths. This maneuver is performed in a continuous motion of the various strikes in an up and down direction. Some Arnis instructors have divided the system into the high, middle and low sinawali. However, it consists only of the two most basic strikes: the forehand strike and the backhand strike. Both are performed by the same hand, giving it the term "single *sinawali*."

Single Weave (Isahang Sinawali)

Double Weave (Dalawang Sinawali)

In the double *sinawali*, the forehand and the backhand strikes are performed by two alternating hands to complete the maneuver.

Double Weave - High, Low, Medium Sequence

Double Weave - High and Low Alternating

FIGURE-8 (PIGURANG OTSO) MANEUVERS

Forehand

Backhand

Backhand

Forehand

This classical maneuver may be performed with a single stick or double sticks. When using double sticks, either hand may be used to perform this maneuver:

- One at a time;
- Both hands at the same time (by the ambidextrous), or;
- One hand going clockwise while the other hand goes counter-clockwise;
- Both hands going in the same direction at the same time.

This continuous circular maneuver, which forms the figure eight, is characterized by changing the position of the wrist depending on the direction of the strike, and making the strike either forehand or backhand. The figure eight *(pigurang otso)* is the foundation of the *redonda*.

ROUNDABOUT (REDONDA) MANEUVERS

The redonda is a continuous circular maneuver that criss-crosses the body and effectively blocks an opponent's strikes. This technique offers multiple circular strikes intended to confuse the opponent. It is designed to inflict multiple strikes against a single opponent or to engage multiple opponents at one time.

CHAPTER 8

THE THREE STAGES OF IMPACT TRAINING

alpok means "impact" and *salpukan* or "impact training" is a type of training without a partner except one's sticks or another training medium. *Salpukan* may be performed with two sticks or against a stationary target. When using two sticks, one is used to strike, while the other is used as a target. The roles of the stick change as you go through the different exercises. There are three stages in impact training: skill development drills, volume of blows or maneuvers, and striking while in motion or demonstration. These are explained below.

STAGE 1 – PAGSASANAY: SKILL DEVELOPMENT DRILLS

There are no advance techniques in Filipino martial arts. What some call advance techniques are actually just basic techniques performed in a superior manner. In order for a technique to be performed in a superior manner, one must train and execute it repeatedly in drills (*pagsasanay*), maneuvers (*pamamaraan*) and demonstrations (*palabas*). Continuous drills guarantee continuous development and improvement in the skills upon which the drills are focused. However, training in the fundamentals must be done to make the trainee aware of each technique's specific application in the overall scheme of things.

Remember that the whole equals to the sum of the parts. For the most efficient teaching and learning process, each technique must be broken down into elements and minute skills. Stick fighting is a complex skill. In learning a complex skill, one must begin with a framework or an orientation towards a goal. Then learn the action patterns one at a time, and, finally, develop the techniques into a system as they become incorporated into the framework.

This stage of training is called impact training and is executed in a pre-arranged sequence. Drills and maneuvers are done without a partner except for the two sticks you train with. Demonstration, however, is done with a partner although the techniques and movements are still structured.

Drills are structured repetition of the same technique over and over again until it becomes a natural reflex action or a simple reaction. It is an action taken without conscious effort or thought. Your target is the stick you hold in front of you. Hold the target stick with your left hand when you strike with the right hand and vice-versa. In this phase of training, you aim for speed, power and accuracy simultaneously. However, avoid loss of control (accuracy) by concentrating too much on power or speed.

The most important factor in this aspect of training is visualization. In conjunction with the direction of placement, focus on the strike's target, usually your target stick. When you focus on the target, the body tends to automatically position itself. Do not move mechanically, rather always move like your life is on the line because at some time, it may very well be.

Drills training must always be regarded as a preparation for a life or death confrontation. Take the stance and posture you normally assume based on your training and techniques. Again, always visualize your opponent by concentrating on your target stick.

Drills training starts with the four quadrant strikes (X pattern). For easy reference, place an imaginary number on the pattern going clockwise: put number 1 as the left top point, number 2 as the right top point, number 3 as the bottom right point, and number 4 as the bottom left point.

Assume a right fighting stance and visualize your opponent also in a right fighting stance. Slide diagonally forward without changing stance. Deliver a right forehand strike on your target stick (held by the left hand), and visualize it as your opponent's left temple. Slide back to the original position. Repeat the process, over and over again, until you can slide quickly, hit with all your power, *bunyaw* as you strike and withdraw smoothly without conscious effort. You must visualize your opponent going down when you strike.

Assume a right fighting stance and visualize your opponent also on a right fighting stance. Slide diagonally forward without changing your stance. Deliver a right backhand strike on your target stick (held by the left hand) visualizing it as your opponent's right temple. Slide back to the original position. Repeat the process over and over again until you can slide quickly, hit with all your power, *bunyaw* as you strike and withdraw smoothly without conscious effort. You must visualize your opponent going down when you strike in this drill as well.

Assume a right fighting stance and visualize your opponent also on a right fighting stance. Slide diagonally forward. Without changing stance, deliver a right forehand strike on your target stick (hold it upside down with your left hand) and visualize it as your opponent's inside right knee. Slide back to the original position. Repeat the process over and over again until you can slide quickly, hit with all your power, *bunyaw* as you strike and withdraw smoothly without conscious effort. You must visualize your opponent going down when you strike.

Assume a right fighting stance and visualize your opponent also in a right fighting stance. Slide diagonally forward without changing your stance. Deliver a right backhand strike on your target stick (hold it upside down with your left hand) and visualize it as your opponent's outside right knee. Slide back to the original position. Repeat the process over and over until you can slide quickly, hit with all your power, *bunyaw* as you strike and withdraw smoothly without conscious effort. You must visualize your opponent going down when you strike.

The next phase is changing to left fighting stance and repeating the same exercises listed in the previous paragraphs. After mastery of the strikes from a regular stance (front leg is the same as the leading hand), execute the techniques from a reverse stance (rear leg is the opposite of the leading hand). Hold the target stick with the leading hand and strike with the reverse hand. Advance to the next stage by stepping forward and stepping backward in one count. Also, train while moving in a clockwise motion and in a counter-clockwise motion.

Rotate the sequence and the combination of the techniques based on the four angles of strikes (multiplication (X) pattern and addition (+) pattern) with the thrusts to the carotid artery, the heart and the liver. After mastery of the X strikes and the + strikes you will have mastered the octagon (eight points strike), which is a combination of the X and the + strikes.

There is no set time limit in this drills training. The gauge one must go by is the progress and proficiency of the student. There are some students who may master the drills training in matters of weeks or months, and there are some who may take longer. The maneuvers training phase follows the drills training phase.

STAGE 2 – PAMAMARAAN: MANEUVERS TRAINING

In the maneuvers training, every basic strike is combined with other strikes such as fanning strikes, weaving strikes, spiral strikes or a combination of all types of strikes. In this stage of training (volume of blows), the student learns how to strike continuously without giving the opponent the opportunity to recover or regain composure.

In the maneuvers impact training, you interchange your target stick with the regular standard length stick and the tungkli (a 5-feet to 6-feet pole). Unlike the regular *baston* (stick) with an approved standard length, the *tungkli* at this time still has no standard dimension. Each school has their own dimension, but five feet to six feet in length and about 1½ inch to 2 inches in diameter is the accepted norm. The gauge of the length and the diameter is the hand size and height of the practitioner.

When using the *tungkli* as target, you hold it at the middle so you can hit with an upward strike or a downward strike without changing the position of the stick. All the exercises in the drills impact training are repeated.

The student is inspired to be creative and imaginative. Picture in your mind all the possible scenarios and train accordingly. There should be no limitation in maneuvers impact training, either in technique or location. Remember, not all encounters happen in the gym or street where you are free to move.

   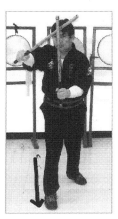

Confined space training and uneven terrain must always be considered. Like the proverbial Boy Scout's motto, you must always be *laging handa* ("always be prepared"). Impact training enables the student to practice his techniques in the privacy of his own space (a room or anywhere he chooses) without a partner and still experience the feel of exchanging blows.

As notes earlier, instructors who profess to be doctrinal and pragmatic are sometimes unimaginative and close-minded. Holding on to the old tradition of learning stick fighting by hitting each other from the first day of training, (because that is how the old masters taught) causes students to lose patience because they do not understand the purpose.

Boxers train in shadow boxing to improve their techniques. In the 3rd World Karate Championships, part of the Philippine's National Karate Team's training was performing hundreds of repetitions of a sweeping block, a front kick, and a reverse punch in front of a mirror to polish their form. A ping pong master once said that he trains his forehand strike and backhand strike thousands of times in front of a large mirror to perfect his form. This is the philosophy behind this type of training.

STAGE 3 - PALABAS: STRIKING WHILE IN MOTION

The third stage of impact training is called *palabas* (demonstration) wherein the student has a training partner instead of a target stick. This training is not sparring but an exercise to allow the student to move while striking.

Initially, only one strike at a time (going through the X and then the + sequence) is delivered. One moves clockwise while the other moves counter-clockwise. Both trainees execute the same technique and hit each other's stick. To the uninitiated, the trainees look like they are fighting, but, in reality, they are just executing strikes simultaneously. After mastery of the single strike, they move on to combining the strikes.

Enterprising instructors use the *palabas* training as a gimmick to entice people to enroll in their class. To make it more fascinating, the "defender" (normally the instructor or a senior student) is blindfolded. At one point in their training, both the "attacker" and the "defender" *must be* blindfolded. One of the downsides to this kind of training is both students develop similar cadence or rhythm instead of their own individual timing. There is no other way of teaching or learning. Martial arts education does not only teach how to execute a technique skillfully, but also to understand how to skillfully execute a technique.

PART 3

EVOLUTION TO PROGRESSIVE TECHNIQUES

The weapon developed by the Philippine natives was used for cutting and hacking. The weapon was big and heavy but very efficient. However, due to its size and weight, it was difficult to maneuver and to use for successive strikes. This seemingly negative characteristic of the native's weapon, however, resulted in the development of the principle of "one-strike, one-kill." Dictated by the design of the weapon, the two most probable strikes were the diagonal downward cuts. It is safe to assume that the original basic Filipino martial arts strikes are the forehand and the backhand. The weapon was designed based on the use, and the technique was developed based on the design of the weapon.

In comparison, the Spaniard's weapon was designed for thrusting. It was light and very maneuverable. Influenced by the European foil and saber weapons and by techniques from other countries, the Filipino weaponry underwent a design change. With the change in design, came a change and development of techniques. When the weapon was redesigned, it became easier to wield. Other strikes and thrusts became less cumbersome to execute and apply. The lighter weapon also required less effort to deliver a continuous maneuver.

CHAPTER 9

THE STRIKES OF ARNIS DE MANO

When the live blade was replaced by sticks and other impact weapons, the techniques were further expanded to conform to the change of the weapon. Soon, more strikes were added and new schools were developed and named after their proprietary maneuvers.

There is a system that employs five strikes. There is a system that employs seven strikes. Still there is a system that calls itself the *otso tiros* or eight strikes. However, the most common style has an expanded to 12 strikes.

Without any reference to any particular school or style, but in the interest of FMA Education of Arnis de Mano shared fundamentals, we present the following information:

- Original natural four strikes (diagonal strikes)
- Acquired four vertical and horizontal strikes
- Basic strikes as offensive or defensive action
- Basic strikes, defensive action, and counter strike
- Elementary — seven strikes system
- Major eight strikes system
- Expanded twelve strikes system
- Advance thirteen strikes system

There are schools that give a number to their target and their strikes and thrusts. Shown in this illustration is the number application when you lead with your right hand.

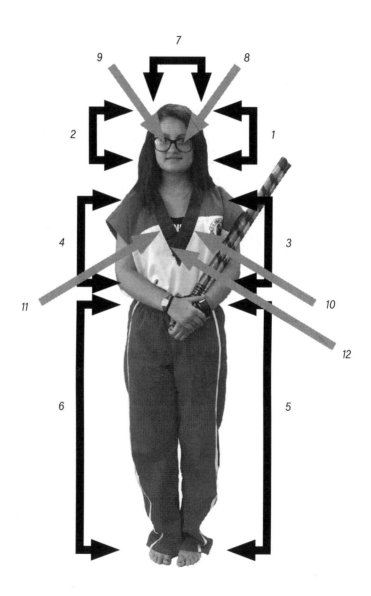

Original Four Diagonal Strikes

1a. Striking technique to the left temple

1b. Forehand strike to the left temple

2a. Striking technique to right temple

2b. Backhand strike to right temple

3a. Striking technique to the left leg

3b. Forehand strike to the left leg

4a. Striking technique to the right leg

4b. Backhand strike to the right leg

Acquired Four Vertical and Horizontal Strikes

1a. Striking technique to the top of the head

1b. Forehand strike to the top of the head

2a. Striking technique to the groin

2b.Backhand strike to the groin

3a. Striking technique to the left arm

3b. Forehand strike to the left arm

4a. Striking technique to the right arm

4b. Backhand strike to the right arm

Elementary Seven Strikes (Right hand lead)

1a. Striking technique to the left temple

1b. Forehand strike to the left temple

2a. Striking technique to right temple

2b. Backhand strike to right temple

3a. Striking technique to the left arm

3b. Forehand strike to the left arm

4a. Striking technique to the right arm

4b. Backhand strike to the right arm

5a. Striking technique to the left leg

5b. Forehand strike to the left leg

6a. Striking technique to the right leg

6b. Backhand strike to the right leg

7a. Striking technique to the top of the head

7b. Forehand strike to the top of the head

There are some schools that do not incorporate the thrusts in their striking system and consider thrusts as a different maneuver altogether.

Major Eight Strikes

There are several schools that adopted eight striking techniques and also give "number names" to the different strikes based on the target. Closer examination reveals that these are still the two basic strikes—the forehand and the backhand strikes applied to different targets.

1a. Striking technique no. 1 to left temple

1b. Forehand strike to left temple

2a. Striking technique no. 2 to right temple

2b. Backhand strike to right temple

3a. Striking technique no. 3 to left knee

3b. Forehand strike to left knee

4a. Striking technique no. 4 to right knee

4b. Backhand strike to right knee

5a. Thrusting technique no. 5 upward thrust to abdomen or solar plexus

5b. Striking technique no. 5 thrust to abdomen

6a. Thrusting technique no. 6
thrust to the left eye or left chest

6b. Forehand thrust to the left
eye or left chest

7a. Thrusting technique no. 7 thrust
to the right eye or right chest

7b. Striking technique no. 7 thrust
to right eye

8a. Forehand strike no. 8 strike to
the top of the head

8b. Forehand strike to the top
of head

Expanded Twelve Strikes

1a. Strike to the left temple

1b. Forehand strike to the left temple

2a. Strike to the right temple

2b. Backhand strike to the right temple

3a. Striking technique to the left arm

3b. Forehand strike to the left arm

4a. Striking technique to the right arm

4b. Backhand strike to the right arm

5a. Middle thrust the abdomen

5b. Forehand thrust to the abdomen

6a. Thrust to the left chest

6b. Forehand thrust to the left chest

7a. Thrust to the right chest

7b. Backhand thrust to the right chest

8a. Striking technique to the right knee

8b. Backhand strike to the right knee

9a. Striking technique to the left knee

9b. Forehand strike to left knee

10a. Thrust to the left eye

10b. Forehand thrust to the left eye

11a. Thrust to the right eye

11b. Backhand thrust to the right eye

12a. Striking technique to the top of the head

12b. Forehand strike to the top of the head

Advanced Thirteen Strikes

1a. Striking technique to the left temple

1b. Forehand strike to the left temple

2a. Striking technique to the right knee

2b. Backhand strike to the right knee

3a. Striking technique to the right temple

3b. Backhand strike to the right temple

4a. Striking technique to the left knee

4b. Forehand strike to the left knee

5a. Thrust to the left chest

5b. Forehand thrust to the left chest

6a. Thrust to the right chest

6b. Backhand thrust to the right chest

7a. Strike to the groin

7b. Forehand strike to the groin

8a. Striking technique to the top of head

8b. Forehand strike to the top of the head

9a. Forehand strike to right temple

9b. Backhand abaniko strike to right temple

10a/b. Forehand abaniko strike to left temple

11a/b. Backhand strike to right knee

12a/b. Forehand strike to left knee

13a/b. Cross Step left behind right foot, backhand abaniko strike to the face

Note: Abaniko strikes of techniques 9 and 10 must be executed in one continuous motion.

PART 4

THE PATTERNS OF FUNDAMENTAL TRAINING

A *becedario* is a Spanish term that means ABCs. In Arnis de Mano, this refers to the fundamentals (ABCs) of the art. The *balangkas ng abece-dario* is a compilation of techniques and maneuvers consistent with the principles and laws of motion explained in Part 1 of this book. For a deeper understanding of the *balangkas*, each individual technique must be expanded on. The transition from forehand to backhand, from overhand to underhand, from linear to circular, from pushing to pulling, from turning to twisting, and vice-versa must be clearly understood.

For a better appreciation of *abecedario*, the *balangkas* are presented in both regular and reverse orientation. Likewise, application of each maneuver, in both regular and reverse orientations is shown. Be creative in performing the *abecedario*. Accompany your performance with music, either drum or cymbals, to enhance the timing and rhythm.

CHAPTER 10

TEACHING AND LEARNING THE ABECEDARIO

There is no written history of the Filipino martial arts. What is now the accepted history is a collection of anecdotes and oral histories handed down from generation to generation, with each generation infusing their own family's views, values, beliefs and personal virtues and faults. This lack of written record makes the history of the fighting arts "iffy" at best, but generally accepted. It is the closest and most credible explanation. The only written account that supports this theory is Pigafetta's journal about the circumnavigation of the world by the Spanish explorer Ferdinand Magellan. In it he writes of "schools" called *bothoan* in the Phillipines where the art of warfare was taught along with with reading and writing.

HISTORY OF THE ABECEDARIOS

In his book, *Amara Arkanis Sistemang Praksiyon: Filipino Martial Arts Education*, Louelle Lledo offered the following account of the history and development of abecedario.

It is generally believed that the Spaniards prohibited the possession of fighting weapons and banned the practice in the fighting arts with the widespread Spanish colonization of

the Philippines, starting approximately in 1565, with the arrival of Legazpi, to 1898 when Philippine Independence was declared by General Emilio Aguinaldo in Kawit, Cavite.

This led to the development of "two systems" of Filipino martial arts. Masters who fled to the mountains further developed the "one-strike, one-kill" system that relied heavily on cutting and hacking movements with live blades, dictated by the configuration of the Filipino fighting blades. This system evolved into the *kruzada* maneuver. Live blade encounters were surmised to be the result of this kind of training. Furthermore, by infusing their paganistic rituals, such as the belief in amulets, charms and magical incantations, their system of fighting became known as "esoteric school." Living an austere, Spartan life in seclusion like hermits, and subsisting off the land, they devised ways to train and develop their techniques through drills and exercises.

Techniques designed for combat were combined in logical arrangements of defensive and offensive maneuvers in sequences. The most noteworthy result of these drills and maneuvers was the development of the *abecedario*, a coherent and methodical organization of these techniques. The *abecedario* is the formulation of ideas, procedures, and transition from one maneuver to the other against the *kruzada* strikes and later on, the *sinko tiros*. The integral composition of *abecedario* are the basic techniques such as the forehand strike, the backhand strike, the overhand thrust, and the underhand thrust. Other techniques include the two patterns of motion, namely the line and the circle, the basis of disarming, the arm turn and the arm twist and the principles of breaking opponent's balance by pushing or pulling. This gave and left the impression that the *abecedario* is a part of "esoteric" Arnis de Mano.

In the 1560s, the masters who stayed in the towns and cities were influenced by the introduction of the *comedya* (Spanish play) depicting battles between the Christians (Europeans) and the Moorish kingdoms of the Middle East. The traditional aspect of this theater form was daring swordfights in violent confrontations. The *comedya* was locally known to Filipinoas as *moro-moro*. Unfortunately, the Spaniards always won in these mock battles. Europeans, by virtue of their Christian religion, claimed to be a superior race with a better fighting art and were therefore better warriors.

The introduction of *moro-moro* gave masters of the Filipino martial arts the opportunity to practice their art openly, in a theatrical platform, using sticks instead of live blades. They introduced techniques influenced by *florete* (European-style epee and foil fencing) such as the straight up and down vertical strikes, the horizontal side-to-side strikes, the circular strikes, and the forward thrusts. These techniques enriched the Filipino martial arts and later evolved into classical maneuvers such as the *sinawali, rompida, redonda, doblete, banda y banda, abaniko* and many others called by different names (Spanish and vernacular) but from the same root. This led to the "birth" of the "classical theatrical" system of fighting arts, which heavily influenced the native system of fighting and helped form present-day Arnis de Mano. The most significant development is the adding of the forward thrust to the *kruzada*, giving birth to the *sinko tiros*.

For lack of what to call each technique, it was given the numeral designation of *"uno-dos-tres-kuatro-sinko"* (one, two, three, four, five). The system was also called *sinko bokales* and used the five vowels or limang patinig "A E I O U," as the name of each technique.

With the Spaniards' acceptance of rattan and wooden sticks, instead of live blades, masters who hid in the mountains came out in the open. They brought with them their "brand" of fighting. Their belief in amulets and magical incantations, still part of their "esoteric art" remained, but from nature worship, they replaced the stones and other natural objects with images and icons of their newfound Christian faith. Even the magical incantations were replaced with Latin and Spanish ones.

The use of the sticks signaled the demise of the widespread practice of live blades. Terms, such as eskrima, estokada, brokil, and, of course, arnis emerged. The Spaniards, however, gave the fighting arts the generic term, Armas de Mano, and then later Arnes de Mano, which eventually evolved into the Filipinized Arnis de Mano. With the passage of time, the two systems merged into one system adopting all the techniques. This is the system now known as Arnis de Mano.

Unfortunately, there were schools that did not accept the practice of the *abecedario*, treating it as an "esoteric" performance instead of a systematic exercise for proficiency.

Filipino's ingenuity in forming new combinations or applications of ideas and principles, once more resulted in the division of the arts, and this time into different schools and styles with different names but similar and identical contents. The influence of European-style and other countries' swordplay further enriched the Filipino art of stick fighting, and made it the premier internationally recognized fighting art it is today.

The merging of the "esoteric schools" with the "classical schools" resulted in the development of the three stages of *abecedario* (fundamentals) against the *sinko tiros* (five strikes): the *defensa natural* (natural defense), the *defensiva ofensiva* (defensive offense,) and the *contra ofensiva* (counter offense).

NATIONWIDE SKILL IN BLADED WEAPONS

Questions have risen about how it was possible that wherever the invading Spaniards went, they witnessed the fighting skill of the natives using the swords (*kalis* or cutlas). On April 27, 1521, Ferdinand Magellan was defeated at the hands of Rajah Lapu-lapu and his men, who were experts in bladed weapons, like the sword and spear.

In February 1564 as Miguel Lopez de Legazpi landed in Abuyog, Leyte, he was greeted by festive natives displaying their skill in bladed weapons. In March of the same year, when they moved to Camiguin Island, natives of the island entertained the foreigners by showing their skill in the use of the sword. In Bohol, they also witnessed the sword wielding ability of the natives.

When the Spaniards moved up north to Luzon, the *mandirigma* (warriors) of Rajah Lakandula and Rajah Soliman, surprised Martin de Goiti and Juan de Salcedo with their *kalis* (sword) skills. The ability of the Filipinos to use the sword (*kalis*), despite being separated by bodies of water with no sea-going ships for regular transport to and from one island to another, can best be explained by Pigafetta when he wrote about the existence of the bothoan schools where the fighting arts were taught with reading and writing. An excellent summary of this is found in Mark Wiley's classic work, *Filipino Martial Culture*.

In 1764, Simon de Anda y Salazar banned the practice of all fighting arts. From the time of Lakandula and Soliman to the time of Andres Bonifacio, the techniques of the fighting arts were secretly passed from one generation to the next.

In 1872, the first successful revolution against Spain took place in Imus, Cavite, and ended with the declaration of the Philippines' independence from Spain on June 12, 1898.

In 1896, after 134 years, arnis de mano was finally allowed to be taught openly when Jose de Azas opened the *Tanghalan ng Sandata* in Manila. Ateneo de Manila also taught arnis de mano with European fencing.

During the Second World War, the Filipino live blade once more saw action. This time the blade technique were referred to as *tabak* or *gulok*. Soldiers who were trained in the use of the *tabak* formed the Bolo Regiment made up of Tabak Battalions. Guerillas, such as Delfin Bernarte, also used live blades against the Japanese. In Bernarte's case, he fabricated his own blades, the *media-luna*, and the *dahong-palay*.

After the war, the Filipino fighting arts or FMA (Filipino martial arts) as it is now called was taught openly in commercial schools and educational institutions. In 1957, Placido Yambao and Buenaventura Mirafuente published a book titled, *Mga Karunungan sa Larong Arnis*. Several books by different

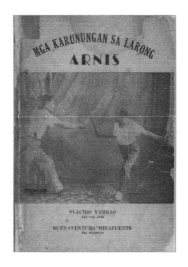

authors followed. At last count, there are more than 100 different books published on arnis de mano and related arts. There also are hundreds more schools and styles than books.

In this section, we present the only known and original pattern or formal exercise of arnis de mano as it was developed by the ancient masters. "Modern masters" have developed and teach other forms based on foreign martial arts.

As a carry-over from the book *Mga Karunungan sa Larong Arnis*, most of the newly-developed forms are called *anyo*. In their book, Yambao and Mirafuente present several anyos which they called *Abakada ng Apat na Taga* up to *Abakada ng Labingdalawang Taga*. The term *anyo*, however, is a misnomer and based on what they want to portray, and is an inappropriate designation. *Anyo*, means "feature," as in the features or looks of a person. In the 1960s, the Institute of National Language approved the term *balangkas* as the accurate term to convey the meaning of techniques patterns in a Sikaran treatise authored by Meliton Geronimo and Emmanuel Querubin.

Daniel Rendal and Delfin Bernarte argue that there is no need to "reinvent the wheel." Both are firm believers of the ingenuity in the development of the *abecedario*, and maintain that the *balangkas ng abecedario* answers the need for a complete set of drills that encompass the defensive and offensive application of arnis de mano techniques and maneuvers. There is no required weapon to perform *abecedario*. *Doble baston* (double sticks), *solo baston* (single stick), *espada y daga* (sword and stick), other alternative weapons, and even empty hands are applicable in all the maneuvers *of abecedario*. This is because Arnis de Mano is characterized by the capability to adapt to new, changing or different requirements.

Each technique, whether defensive or offensive or both simultaneously, may be executed in a regular or reverse orientation. The *defensa natural* (natural defense) has a fixed pattern designed to cover all angles of attack. In addition, one must be trained in the prescribed sequence. The maneuvers, the transition from one technique to the other and the footwork must follow the set form. The *defensa ofensiva* (defensive offense) and the *contra ofensiva* (counter offense) have no prescribed maneuvers allowing the arnisador to apply his best technique in a simple reaction.

Thanks to Miguel Zubiri, in 2009, the Republic Act 9850 ("Arnis Law") was signed into law declaring Arnis de Mano as the Official National Martial Art of the Philippines. It is now mandatory to include Arnis de Mano as part of the physical education curriculum in all grade levels in the educational system.

In 2010, several teachers joined and formed the Mataw Guro Association Filipino Martial Arts Education for Arnis de Mano. Their mission is to elevate Arnis de Mano into an accredited Filipino Martial Arts Education.

We present *abecedario* in regular and reverse orientation in this handbook using *doble baston*. To see the beauty and applicability of *abecedario*, the student is encouraged and challenged to use *solo baston, espada y daga*, empty hands, alternative weapons and whatever is available and can be used as a weapon.

Regular Orientation of the Depensa Natural

Preparatory on-guard position

1. Lastiko Retirada

2. Kruzada Diretso

3. Plantsada

4. Pinayungan

5. Palis Abierta

6. Estrella Seguida

7. Kruzada Palihis

8. Aldabis

9. Media Fraile

10. Palis Cerrada

11. Bartikal

12. Tumbada Kruzada

13. Aldabon

14. Arabis

15. Sombrada Cerrada

16. Sombrada Abierta   17. Pluma   18. Romper   19. Sablig

20. De Kadena   21. Kadena Real   22. Panipis Abierta   23. Panipis Cerrada

24. O'ekis Abierta   25. O'ekis Cerrada

Note: Originally numbers 24 and 25 are intermediary or transition strikes counted as one technique.

The *defensa natural abecedario* is a sight to behold when executed by a skillful practitioner. The footwork in the transition, the continuity of the motion from one technique to the other, and the hip movement make it a beautiful dance. When combined with the *abaniko* technique after each maneuver and timed-with the banging sticks in rhythm with the music of the agong, the abecedario is quite a spectacle. The beauty of the art, hidden in dance form was never regarded by the Spanish authorities as a fighting art, and it allowed the old masters to train in the open.

Reverse Orientation of Depensa Natural

Preparatory on-guard position

1. Lastiko Retirada

2. Kruzada Diretso

3. Plantsada

4. Pinayungan

5. Palis Abierta

6. Estrella Seguida

7. Kruzada Palihis

8. Aldabis

9. Media Fraile

10. Palis Cerrada

11. Bartikal

12. Tumbada Kruzada

13. Aldabon

14. Arabis

15. Sombrada Cerrada

16. Sombrada Abierta

17. Pluma

18. Romper

19. Sablig

20. De Kadena

21. Kadena Real

22. Panipis Abierta

23. Panipis Cerrada

24. O'ekis Abierta

25. O'ekis Cerrada

*Back to on-guard
position*

Application of Reverse Orientation Abecedario

Defensa Natural	Defensa Ofensiva	Contra Ofensiva

1. Lastiko Retirada

2. Kruzada Diretso

3. Plantsada

4. Pinayungan

5. Palis Abierta

6. Estrella Seguida

7. Kruzada Palihis

8. Aldabis

9. Media Fraile

10. Palis Cerrada

11. Bartikal

12. Tumbada Kruzada

13. Aldabon

14. Arabis

15. Sombrada Abierta

16. Sombrada Cerrada

17. Pluma

18. Romper

19. Sablig

20. De Kadena

21. Kadena Real

22. Panipis Abierta

23. Panipis Cerrada

24. O'ekis Abierta

25. O'ekis Cerrada

Back To On-Guard Position

PART 5

KARUNUNGANG LIHIM (KALI) NG ARNIS DE MANO

Before the Spanish colonization of what is now the Philippines, there was supposedly a book known as *Aklat ng Karunungang Lihim* ("Secret Book of Wisdom") that deals with ethics, reading, writing, arithmetic and the art of warfare. It is also known as *Aklat ng Limang Katangian* or the ("Secret Book of Five Attributes").

At first, the natives tried to conceal the existence of the book from the Spaniards. Considering the book to be just a part of the paganistic practice, the Spaniards ignored the book but gave it the Spanish name *Libro del Cinco Attibuto* and later *Libro del Cinco Vocales* ("Book of Five Vowels"). When the Philippines were liberated from Spanish rule and enjoyed freedom to use their native language, the book was renamed *Libro ng Sinko Tiros*. Those who still wanted to give the book a veil of secrecy called it *Aklat ng Limang Patinig*, the translation of *Libro del Cinco Vocales*. When Daniel Rendal, an educator by profession, wrote about this book, the title he used was *The Book of Five Attributes*. In Filipino, it was translated to *Aklat ng Limang Katangian*.

The information in this chapter is based on the writings, teachings and philosophies of Daniel Rendal and Delfin Bernarte.

CHAPTER 11

THE TWO SIDES OF THE ARNIS DE MANO

Rendal explained the contents of the book, and emphasized there really is no mystery about the book. In his simple explanation, he said that the Filipino martial art is like a coin with two sides. One side deals with the physical aspects of the art and the other deals with the spiritual aspects of the art. The two cannot be separated, but are independent of each other. The physical aspects are the *sinko tiros* or five strikes: right or left forehand downward strike, right or left backhand downward strike; right or left forehand upward strike; right or left backhand upward strike, and right or left forward thrust. The simplicity and affectivity of *sinko tiros* became the basic system of several schools with some even naming their schools or system as Sinkos Tiros (or Cinco Teros in Spanish).

The other side of the coin, deals with the spiritual aspects. *KArunungan LIhim* ("secret wisdom," the "real" KA-LI) of Arnis de Mano is like a coin. It is one entity that has two sides that make up the coins. The sides cannot be separated, and although it is independent of each other, it makes up the coin. In Filipino, the sides are called *kara* or *krus*. In English, it is head or tail. In Arnis de Mano, one side is the concept and the other the actualization. The concept is referred to by many names. It is called *cinco vocales, limang patinig*, the five attitudes, and the five attributes. In the system of systems, it has been simplified as the pentagonal foundation. Although there are many names, they are all of equal importance. The other side is called *cinco tiros* or five strikes. There are many variations and modifications of the *cinco tiros* that resulted in classical maneuvers, including for example, the *sinawali, the kruzada*, the *ginunting*, the *abaniko*, and the *redonda*. These variations were achieved by modifying the maneuver with the two directions of motion: linear and circular. This section explains the concept of the coin in detail.

DANIEL RENDAL: KUATRO PUNTAS KRUZADA

In the 1920s, Daniel Rendal, an educator from Cebu, developed his own style of Arnis de Mano, which he called Kuatro Puntas Kruzada. When he relocated to Manila, he established a school called the Cebu School of Self-Defense, where he taught Combat Judo, Arnis, and saber fencing. Combat Judo was the term the U.S. military used for unarmed combat. Arnis is the stick-fighting

art that became very popular. Saber Fencing was an English translation of Eskrima, a carryover of the art as it was called in Cebu where Rendal learned the art of the bladed weapon.

During the Second World War, Rendal joined the guerilla movement in Rizal Province, making good use of his expertise in the use of bladed weapons. After the war, he established his residence in Baryo Kuli-kuli in Makati, Rizal. Kuli-kuli was still heavily forested at that time, and it was a favorite camping and bivouac area for Boy Scouts, ROTC and some military units. It was not too far from "civilization," but offered the feel of being in the middle of a jungle. Here, Rendal taught some military personnel (both American and Filipino) who were assigned in a detachment near his residence.

Through an uncle who was with Rendal in the guerilla movement, Emmanuel Querubin was referred and accepted as a student. Sometimes they trained at Rendal's residence in Kuli-kuli, which was fast becoming urbanized; and sometimes they trained in Pasay where Querubin has his Sikaran school. When Kuli-kuli was transformed into a commercial area, Querubin lost contact with Rendal but not before Rendal entrusted to him his writings that explained his art and the philosophies and principles of Kuatro Puntas Kruzada. It is unfortunate that most of these records were lost or destroyed. Working from memory, Querubin is trying to reconstruct the "Quatro Puntas Kruzada."

Learning the esoteric aspect of Arnis de Mano, Rendal credits his *agimat* (amulet) and *orasyon* (prayer) as his lifesavers during his guerilla encounters in the Second World War. Although he did not talk much about it, Rendal admitted that he swallowed his agimat so it will always be with him. He never showed it to anybody, but described it as black and called it a "moon stone," because according to him it came down from the heavens like a falling star. Could it have been a "tektite?" Querubin has seen several tektites from the collection of Dr. Otley H. Beyer, the famous anthropologist. There was a question that haunted Querubin about the agimat, but he never had the courage to ask Rendal about it. How did he manage to keep the agimat in his body and prevent the course of nature from expelling it?

Next to his *agimat*, Rendal said his most guarded possessions are two Spanish books entitled *Doctrina Christiana en Lengua Española y Tagala* and *Libro Del Cinco Vocales*. It is not clear how and when he acquired these books. He admitted that his orasyon came from the books *Doctrina Christiana en Lengua Española y Tagala* and the *Quatro Puntas Kruzada*, and that his philosophies are based on the concept of the *Libro Del Cinco Vocales*.

In 1958, Daniel Rendal pioneered the use of head protection.

BERNARTE BROKIL: SISTEMANG PRAKSIYON

Sistemang praksiyon (fraction-time system). is a principle and a system born out of extreme necessity and also proven in the battlefield when the Philippines was a pawn in the political game against foreign aggressors. It was first conceived by Pastor Bernarte of Macabebe, Pampanga, but remained a theory and never incorporated into his system of Brokil (Pampanga style of stick fighting). Pastor Bernarte lived through three invading forces. He was born in 1858 during the later days of struggle against the Spaniards. He lived through the American

colonization and the Japanese invasion, and succumbed to natural causes in 1945 at the ripe age of 87.

The Bernarte Brokil fighting art and his theory were passed on by Pastor to his son Delfin Bernarte. Delfin Bernarte further developed and perfected the theory, and incorporated into his fighting maneuvers, calling it Sistemang Praksiyon (Fraction System). He coined the term "Kali," from Karunungan Lihim, which describes his "hit hard, hit fast and hit deep" approach. Born in 1912 in Macabebe, Pampanga, Delfin Bernarte moved his family to Indang, Cavite in 1933. During the Second World War, Delfin Bernate hid in the mountains of Cavite and Batangas, and engaged in guerilla activities against the Japanese.

To protect his family, he lived a hermit's life in the mountains. He became known as the Engkanto (a spirit in Philippine folklore) due to his hit and run raids. People started saying the enemy could not see him because of his *anting-anting* (amulet).

He designed his own weaponry, such as the *medya-luna*, and superstitious townspeople claimed that *Engkanto* was actually an animal due to the injuries he inflicted on the enemy. The design of his weapon allowed him to disembowel, mutilate, and split the body from the groin going up or the sternum going down, and, when he chose, to completely sever the head or cut the body in half. Delfin Bernarte explained that he exacted injuries in varying degrees to mislead the enemy to believe the same man was responsible for these actions. He also claimed it was more demoralizing to the enemies to see their comrade-in-arms half dead, with their entrails hanging out.

Delfin Bernarte's plan to make his son Roberto the next successor to the Sistemang Praksiyon legacy did not materialize. Roberto was more interested in the American-influenced way of life than the Filipino fighting arts. Delfin Bernarte was getting concerned he may take Sistemang Praksiyon with him to the grave. In keeping up with the Filipino fighting art tradition, he was not willing to impart the skill to just anybody outside the family.

In 1970, that all changed. Bernarte met Louelle Lledo, a medical technologist and an officer in the Philippine Air Force Reserves. Lledo and Bernarte's daughter, Flora, were staying in the same boarding house. Louelle Lledo was a rising star in the martial arts of Filipino Sikaran, Japanese Karate and Arnis de Mano. Delfin Bernarte had found a protégé. He trained Louelle Lledo in the Bernarte Brokil Sistemang Praksiyon method. Bernarte imparted in Lledo the skill that was developed and perfected in the battlefield during the Second World War. In 1980, Delfin Bernarte named Louelle Lledo, now the father of Bernarte's three grandchildren, (Louelle and Flora tied the knot of holy matrimony in 1972) heir and successor to the Sistemang Praksiyon heritage. Delfin Bernarte bequeathed his *bahi* (hardwood fighting stick) and allegedly his *anting-anting* to Louelle Lledo. When queried about the *anting-anting*, Louelle Lledo just smiled.

ACTUALIZATION OF THE CINCO VOCALES CONCEPT

We have previously discusses the evolution of the *sinko tiros (cinco teros)* strikes also known as *cinco vicales* (five vowels). In this chapter we would like to expand on the "secret wisdom" inherent in this striking method. The five strikes, following the five intrinsic angles or direction, was given the numeral designation as its name. To conceal the meaning of this numeral designation, the system was also called *cinco vocales* and used the five vowels or *limang patinig* (A E I O U), as the name of each technique.

The *cinco vocales* (five vowels) are also called the "five attitudes." In the system of systems, this concept is better known as the principle of MIBOME (see Part 1 of this book), also referred to as the pentagonal foundation, which stands for spirit, skill, speed, strength, and style. They are interrelated and complement each other. They have equal importance in a strategy or battle. Let us now explain the concept five vowel concept in more depth.

A—A forward thrust to the middle area is designated as A. It is the only technique that is different in execution. It is a straight thrust (*tusok* or *saksak*). Likewise, it is the only letter that stands alone (I being a derivative of E and U being a derivative of O).

A

E—Most *arnisadors* are right handed and lead with the right hand and the right foot, holding the weapon at shoulder level. On account of muscle formation in relation to stance and posture, the first strike the body "wants" to perform is a forehand, downward strike from right to left. This is the strike to the upper left side. If the person is left-handed and leads with the left hand and the left foot, his body will "want" to execute a left, forehand downward strike from left to right. This strike is termed E.

E

I—By moving the center of gravity, a right-handed person who leads with the right hand and the right foot and holds the weapon at shoulder level will "want" to execute a backhand, downward strike from right to right. Likewise a left-handed person who leads with the left hand and the left foot will "want" to strike with a backhand, downward strike from left to left. This strike is termed I, the derivative of E.

I

O—When right-handed person holds his weapon at waist level and leads with the right hand and the right foot, the body "wants" to deliver a forehand upward strike from right to left. If the person is left-handed and leads with the left hand and the left foot, his natural tendency will

O

U

be to execute a left forehand, upward strike from left to right. This strike is termed O.

U—By moving the center of gravity, a right-handed person who leads with the right hand and the right foot and holds the weapon at waist level will "want" to execute a backhand upward strike from right to right. Likewise a left-handed person who leads with the left hand and the left foot will "want" to strike with a backhand upward strike from left to left. This strike is termed U, the derivative of O.

In esoteric Arnis de Mano, each letter of the *limang patinig (cinco vocales)* has its own meaning, corresponding to the five attributes. Likewise, each attribute corresponds to the five elements of earth, water, fire, wind, and nature.

A — AGIMAT

Agimat or *amuleto* in Spanish refers to the *amulet* that the *arnisador* never leaves home without. It represents the earth, the physical attribute that is solid and resistant to movement. It may be anything from a crucifix, a ring, a necklace, a scarf, a shirt, a bandana, or even an ordinary stone that has been infused with "special powers." In the mind, it represents the stability and confident nature of the individual.

E — ESPIRITU

Espiritu in Spanish stands for the spirit, an incorporeal entity that infuses the amulet with "special powers" and protects the owner. Sometimes it is called the *angel dela guardia* or "guardian angel." Like water, it is fluid, flowing, and formless. It is associated with emotion and the personality.

I — ISIP

Intelligencia in Spanish stands for the "brain power" that controls the agimat and the *espiritu.* Like fire, it represents the energetic, forceful motivation and desire to grow. As we grow physically, we grow mentally as well, in our knowledge and experience. It is associated with benevolence, compassion, and wisdom.

O – ORASYON

Oracion in Spanish stands for the sacred incantations that invoke the *espiritu* to give power to the *agimat* to protect the holder from harm and violence. To give the holder the ability and skill to subdue the enemy, no matter how superior the opposing force may be. It is associated with the wind because it grows, expands, and enjoys freedom of movement.

U – UNAWA

Unificar in Spanish stands for the understanding on how all the attributes come together and unite into one, and how to use them effectively for maximum result. It represents things beyond our everyday experience, such as invoking the power to connect to the creative energy of the world. With understanding, a warrior properly attuned with nature can sense their surroundings and act without thinking and even without using their physical senses.

CLASSIFICATIONS OF ARNIS DE MANO

There are typically two classifications of Arnis de Mano, the contemporary, and the classical. The contemporary may be classified into "Combat Arnis" and "Sport Arnis." On the other hand, the classical version may be subdivided, into "Traditional" (sometimes also referred to as cultural) and "Esoteric."

Whatever the classification they are all bound together by three common aspects: part art, part science, and part sports. With the founding of the Mataw Guro Association, it is hoped that they will also be considered part of Filipino martial arts education. However, the priority and purpose of training can still differentiate each classification.

There are schools of Arnis de Mano that concentrate on teaching the art mainly as a means of defense and as a combative art, such as by police agencies and the military. The emphasis of their training is in the combat aspects of Arnis. These schools do not engage in "scoring points" and winning trophies or medals at competitions. To them, Arnis de Mano is used as a strategy to neutralize the opponent to eliminate the threat.

Then, there are schools whose priority is to broaden their following and income by winning trophies and medals in competitions. These schools may be classified as the "sports Arnis schools." To these schools, the gauge of whether the school is good or not is by the number of tournaments they win. To them, Arnis de Mano is 100% about "scoring points" and collecting as many trophies and medals as possible.

"Sports Arnis" is an attempt to keep the "live blade" encounters of the past alive. However, because these confrontations are against the law and against survival instincts, padded sticks and protective gear have taken the place of live blades in an "all-out survival of the fittest" contest. Although the techniques and strategies may be the same as contemporary Arnis, the ideals of classical Arnis de Mano are entirely different.

The traditional Arnis de Mano is part art, part science, and part sports. As an art, Arnis de Mano is a dance form that is uniquely Filipino. Watching a skilled *arnisador* perform the techniques of *abecedario* and other strategies to music is like watching birds in formation while in flight. The graceful transition from one motion to another is both natural and energetic. Style and form in traditional Arnis de Mano is just as important as speed and power, perhaps even more. The laws of physics and motion must govern every movement to achieve style and form. During Arnis gatherings and events, practitioner of traditional Arnis will demonstrate their art rather than compete in tournaments. For them, displaying the grace and beauty of Arnis is like displaying the beauty of a painting or architecture. For them, beauty in the execution of a strategy is more of a sport than trying to knock the life out of the other person.

The least talked about type of Arnis de Mano is the esoteric type. This type is also governed by the three aspects of art, science, and sport, but with the added aspect of spiritualism.

In the olden days, "Esoteric Arnis" with all the combative aspects was likely the most common practice. Before the coming of the Spaniards, the Filipino people's spiritual beliefs were based on nature worship and rituals. Every family had its own talisman or charm (*anting-anting* or *agimat*), which was believed to avert evil and bring good fortune, magic, and miraculous powers. The *anting-anting* or *agimat* came in different forms, shapes, and size. The *orasyon* (incantations) also came in different languages and sounds. With the Christianization of the Philippines, the culture, beliefs, and agimat took on a different character. The most common *agimat* or *anting-anting* came in the form of the crucifix, rosary or scapular, a monastic garmet. Spanish and Latin became the most common language to perform incantations or *orasyons*. *Arnisadors* do not go into a possible confrontation without their *agimat* and *orasyon*. In fact, most do not even step out of their homes without uttering some magical words or rubbing their *agimat*. The Filipinos slowly transitioned their pagan practices to Christian practices as they were converted, and based their *anting-anting* and *orasyon* on their newfound religion. The Latin and Spanish versions of the "Our Father," "Hail Mary" and "Glory Be," became the most common *orasyons*. The crucifix or scapular of the Virgin Mary, worn around the neck, became the most common *anting-anting*.

However, there were still those who still clung to the old tradition and have not changed. Most of these are the *manggamot* (healers), *arbularyo* (herbalist) and *manghihilot* (bonesetter). In addition, those who practice the "healing" arts are adept in the "killing" arts.

In the mid 1960s the military and the police, headed by Valentin de los Santos, massacred the Lapiang Malaya to suppress their uprising. Armed only with bolos and their *anting-anting*, the Lapiang Malaya was no match against M16 and .45 caliber bullets. After this incident, the belief in *anting-anting* and *orasyon*, although still practiced, became less prominent due to "Esoteric Arnis" practitioners' fear of being killed and ostracized.

PART 6

SPORTS ARNIS TOURNAMENT RULES & REGULATIONS

In this chapter we will discuss the rules, regulations and provisions of sports Arnis. This includes tournament officials and their qualifications; duties and functions of administrators and referees, judges and scorekeepers, medical officers and announcers; official attire of officials and contestants; logistical requirtements of the fight area; competitor protective armor and sticks; and other stipulations, conductand competitive events.

CHAPTER 12

SPORTS ARNIS DE MANO TOURNAMENT RULES AND REGULATIONS

ARTICLE ONE: GENERAL PROVISIONS

SECTION 1: PURPOSE

These rules are instituted for ensuring a strict, fair and uniform method of judging, thus enhancing the authority of the tournament officials and the dignity of the competition. Further, it is the aim of these Rules and Regulations to promote, share and enrich the Filipino Fighting Arts and create a venue for cultural exchange and education, and to set the highest standards of amateur athletic competition.

SECTION 2: TOURNAMENT OFFICIALS
- Administrator: Taga-Pangasiwa
- Referee: Taga-Pasiya
- Side Judges: Taga-Hatol
- Official Scorer: Taga-Tala

"No matter how good you think you are rest assured that there is somebody better."

- Official Timer: Taga-Takda
- Medical Officer: Taga-Lunas
- Announcer: Taga-Pahayag
- Tournament Assistant: Katulong

SECTION 3: QUALIFICATIONS OF OFFICIALS

- Thorough knowledge of the Official Tournament Rules and Regulations.

- Ability to conduct and control the contest in a fair, safe and orderly manner.

- Ability to give a professional and fair judgment without regards to personal or other affiliations.

- Pass a written and practical test for the appropriate position conducted by the Technical Committee:

- Administrator must pass the test for administrator, referee, judge, scorekeeper, and timer roles and be able perform any assigned task.

- Referee must pass the tests for referee, judge, scorekeeper, and timer roles and be able to perform any assigned task.

- Judge must pass tests for judge, scorekeeper, and timer roles and be able to perform any assigned task.

- Scorekeeper and timer must pass appropriate tests and be able to perform assigned task.

- Must be a member of good standing with the proper updated accreditation organization.

- Medical officer must be certified to perform first aid, cardio-pulmonary resuscitation (CPR) and proficient in the use of defibrillator equipment.

- Medical officer must be able to inspect and certify that a contestant is physically and mentally capable of competing in the tournament. If possible, contestants must submit a medical certificate to this effect prior to the start of the competition. A medical certificate will be made part of the permanent record of the tournament.

- Ability to keep and maintain records of the tournament.

SECTION 4: DUTIES AND FUNCTIONS

Administrator

- Suspend, discipline and/or disqualify any or all tournament officials for unprofessional and un-sportsmanlike conduct and/or demeanor.
- Act as the arbiter and final authority in the interpretation of the rules and regulations.
- Reverse and/or change the decision of the officials for gross and obvious error in judgment.
- Make sure that all necessary equipment of the officials are available prior to the start of the bout (5 silver whistles with yellow lanyards, 4 red flags, 4 blue flags, official time clock, buzzer or bell, white banner with stand, black banner with stand, score cards, time cards, 3 sets of blue and 3 sets of red protective armors, and 3 pairs of blue padded and 3 pairs of red padded fighting sticks).
- Inspect and approve appropriate protective gear and padded sticks of the contestants prior to the start of the bout.
- Inspect and approve the integrity of the official fight area.
- Be willing and able to serve in any capacity as tournament official.
- Ensure that the tournament is conducted in a fair, safe, and orderly manner.

Referee

- Conduct and control the contest in a sportsmanlike atmosphere and attitude.
- Call the appropriate point for a scoring technique.
- Call a foul for an unacceptable technique. (Refer to Article Two, Section 9)

- Deduct appropriate point(s) for foul techniques. (Refer to Article Two, Section 9)

- Disqualify contestant for unsportsmanlike conduct, such as repeated foul techniques, refusal to obey the orders of the officials, refusal to engage, stalling for time, repeated stepping out of the fight area, and conduct unbecoming of a Filipino martial artist. (Refer to Article Two, Section 9)

- Any player who has been disqualified and expelled for a major violation will be barred for life in a sanctioned tournament. (Refer to Article Two, Section 9)

- Terminate a fight in the case of an injury (Refer to Article 2, Section 9) or other cause (only the referee has the authority to terminate a fight).

- Confirm a score given by a side judge if he agrees and if necessary with the concurrence of the three other judges.

- Contradict a score given by a side judge, and, if necessary, with the concurrence of the three other judges.

- Announce the winner of the bout.

- Decision of the fight officials may be reviewed, reversed and/or changed by the administrator, but only in largely obvious errors in judgment.

- Be willing and able to serve in any other capacity he/she is qualified and certified to hold.

- Insure that the tournament is conducted in a fair, safe and orderly manner.

Side Judge

- Call a score for an effective technique.

- Call the attention of the referee for a foul technique that the referee may have not seen.

- Call the attention of the referee if any of the contestants step out of the fight area.

- Call the attention of the referee to confer with the other side judges for a smooth, clean and sportsmanlike contest.

- Give a judgment at the end of the bout. Be willing and able to serve in any other capacity he/she is qualified and certified to hold.

- Insure that the tournament is conducted in a fair, safe and orderly manner.

Scorekeeper

- Keep a record and tally all the points earned by the players or deducted by the referee.

- Each record must be signed by the referee and counter-signed by the administrator at the end of each bout and be made a permanent record of the tournament.

- All foul, deductions, warnings and disqualification must be noted on the record.

- The scorekeeper cannot score the match.

- Be willing and able to serve in any other capacity he/she is qualified and certified to hold.

- Assist to insure that the tournament is conducted in a fair, safe, and orderly manner.

Official Timer

- Keep a record of the time of a bout, indicating thereon all breaks and timeouts called by the referee.

- Indicate that time is on by placing a white banner on the officiating table.

- Indicate that time is off by placing a black banner on the officiating table.

- Signal with a buzzer or bell the start and the end of the bout.

- Submit the session record to the administrator who will sign it at the end of each bout.

- Make sure the record is attached to the scorekeeper's record and be made part of the permanent record of the tournament organizers.

- The timer cannot score the match.

- Be willing and able to serve in any other capacity he/she is qualified and certified to hold.

- Assist to insure that the tournament is conducted in a fair, safe and orderly manner.

Medical Officer

- Medical officer will be the final authority in determining that an injured player will continue or not continue the fight.

- Medical officer will determine the physical and mental ability of a player to compete in both the Tunggali (sparring) and Balangkas (forms) competitions.

- Medical officer cannot score the match.

- Assist to insure that the tournament is conducted in a fair, safe and orderly manner.

Announcer

- Announce to the public the type of match prior to the start of the bout.

- Introduce the players for each match.

- Announce to the public when the referee gives a score.

- Announce to the public when the referee gives a warning/point deduction/disqualification.

- Announce to the public the winner of the match after the referee gives the decision.

- Announcer cannot score the match.

- Assist to insure that the tournament is conducted in a fair, safe and orderly manner.

Tournament Assistants

- Arrange the players in their proper fighting order and their proper position.

- Assist the players in putting on and removing the protective armor.

- Provide the fighting sticks to the players.

- Make themselves available for errands as may be required by the other officials.

- Tournament assistants cannot score the match.

- Assist to insure that the tournament is conducted in a fair, safe, and orderly manner.

SECTION 5: OFFICIAL ATTIRE

Tournament Officials

- White, short-sleeved *barong tagalog* over a white t-shirt.

- Black trousers.

- Black leather shoes with rubber soles.

- Silver whistle on a yellow lanyard.

Attire of Contestants

- Official club or association uniform.

- For independent contestants, red trousers and a white t-shirt is required.

- White sneaker footwear may be worn (leather shoes or shoes with leather soles are not be allowed).

- Contestants' uniform must be free from all derogatory and discriminatory design that is offensive in nature as per the opinion of the tournament officials.

- Contestants' uniform must be free from all designs and accessories that may cause injury to the contestants, the officials and others.

- Traditional Filipino costume may be worn during competition for forms (*Balangkas*), organized set of drills (*bigayan*), and organized set of offensive and defensive techniques in a prearranged and choreographed system.

- Official protective armor must be worn during *tunggali* (sparring) competitions.

SECTION 6: LOGISTICAL REQUIREMENTS

Official Fight Area
- Twenty-four (24) feet by 24-feet square area with clear markings for borders. Designate and properly identify blue side, red side and front (neutral) that is the designated white side.

- Front side must be oriented to the presidential table (if any) or to the flag (if tournament is held in a foreign country – that country's flag and a flag of the Republic of the Philippines must be raised).

- Fight area must be a flat, level, safe, debris and hazard free area that is preferably a polished wooden floor or a material such as hard rubber or a tatami (Japanese straw) mat.

- Twenty-four (24) inches marks, 8-feet apart for contestants starting points; located approximately in the middle of the fight area.

- A stool in each corner for the judges outside the fight area.

- Three separate officiating tables about 8-feet from the front border and four feet apart.

- The middle table will be for the chief administrator and the medical officer and the side tables will be for the scorekeeper and the timer.

- Tournament assistants must be in the immediate vicinity of the fight area for accessibility.

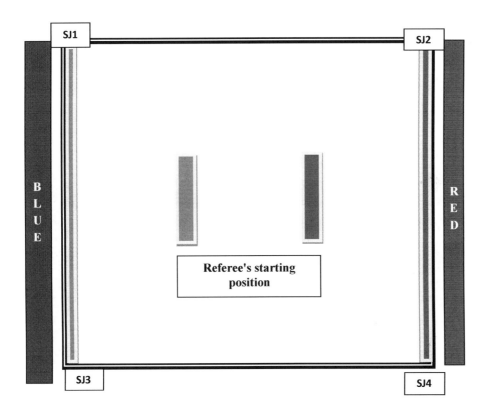

- SJ - Side Judge 1, 2, 3, 4.
- 24-feet by 24-feet with clear markings for borders.
- Fight area must be flat, level, safe and debris-free, preferably polished wooden floor.

Official Protective Armor

- The head protector should be made of a flexible yet sturdy material such as plastic or fiberglass composite (foam rubber inside) with a wire screen mesh for the face and extra ear protection and flaps for the neck area.

- The body protector should be made of flexible material with bamboo or plastic or fiberglass composite strips to protect the shoulders, chest, and sides. It should have protective flaps for the hips and lower abdominal area.

- Gauntlet should be made of flexible material to allow proper gripping of the stick while still providing protection to the arms and hands.

- Thigh, knee, and shin protectors should be made with flexible material with safety strips to protect the thighs, knees and shin bones.
- Protective groin supporter.

Official Fighting Sticks
- Adult and seniors: 30-inches long rattan stick, 1 ¼ inch in diameter and about ¼ inch thick rubber or foam padding.
- Junior: 28-inches long rattan stick, 1 ¼ inch in diameter and about ¼ inch thick rubber or foam padding.
- Minor: 24-inches long rattan stick, 1 ¼ inch in diameter and about ¼ inch thick rubber or foam padding.
- 12-inches short rattan stick, 1 ¼ inch in diameter and about ¼ inch thick rubber or foam padding.
- Ends of sticks must also be covered with rubber or foam.

SECTION 7: STIPULATIONS
- The tournament organizers and the officiating panel may jointly authorize the creation and promulgation of rules to meet unusual requirements. However, such rules shall not be in conflict with the official rules and regulations. All rules must be in writing and be made available to all officials and contestants before the start of the competition.
- All persons who elect to compete in any tournament under these rules and regulations do so at their own risk, and realize that the Filipino martial arts competition involves risk of serious physical injury, permanent physical injury or even death and shall not hold the organizers, officials and/or competitors liable or responsible.
- Prior to any competition, participants must sign the entry form, the injury/death waiver, and release all liabilities of the organizers, officials, members, and competitors. Further, the appropriate entry fees and all required identification must be submitted with the entry form.

- Permission is given to any serious practitioner, group, club or association of Arnis de Mano or similar arts to use the tournament rules and regulations in part or in whole, provided proper credit is given in writing to the authors of this book. The authors and publishers of this book, its members, officers, and associates are not held liable or responsible for any injury, damage or death sustained in the course of a tournament.

- Tournament organizers reserve the right to impose disciplinary sanctions, which may include but are not limited to reprimand, disqualification, suspension and/or expulsion, forfeiture of title or honors and any other appropriate disciplinary actions for violations in the use and possession of prohibited substances in the course of the tournament. Other violations that can result in disciplinary action include participants who make fraudulent statements, misrepresent their age or level of training, use an assumed name, commit gross misconduct and un-sportsmanlike behavior and other acts contrary to the recognized principles of the Filipino fighting arts and common norm of decency.

ARTICLE TWO – CONDUCT OF COMPETITION

SECTION 1: TYPES OF BOUTS

There are three types of competition:

1. **Balangkas:** One-man choreographed and organized set of techniques using sticks or other alternative weapons.

2. **Bigayan:** Two-man choreographed and organized, pre-arranged set of armed and unarmed offensive and defensive techniques

3. **Tunggali:** Sparring contest which are subdivided into the following:

   - Solo Baston (single stick)

   - Doble Baston (two sticks)

   - Espada y daga (one long stick and one short stick)

SECTION 2: MATCH CLASSIFICATION

- Male and females are not allowed to compete with each other in Tunggali competitions.

- Bigayan pair may be mixed gender.

- Height will not be a factor in match classifications (for example, a 4-foot fighter may fight against a 6-foot fighter, provided they both are in the same weight classification).

Male weight classification:

- Lightweight — below 140 pounds

- Middleweight — 141 – 170 pounds

- Heavyweight — 171 pounds and above

- Open weight — no weight limitations

Female weight classification:

- Lightweight — below 120 pounds

- Middleweight — 121 – 150 pounds

- Heavyweight — 151 and above

- Open weight — no weight limitations

Weigh-ins and weight classification will be done prior to the tournament

Level of skill classification for both for males and females will not be based on grade or belt but by the length of training:

- Beginner: 1 day to 1 year of training

- Novice: 1 to 2 years of training

- Intermediate: 2 to 3 years of training

- Advanced: 3 years + training

Any competitor who declares his or her level of training will be deemed to be at that level of experience and will not be allowed to participate in a lower level of experience in any future tournament

Age classification for both males and females are as follows:

- Minor: 15 to 17 years old
- Junior: 18 to 25 years old
- Adult: 26 to 40 years old
- Senior: 41 years and above

Any competitor who declares his or her age classification will be deemed to be at that age classification and will not be allowed to participate in a lower age classification in any future tournaments. Nobody under the age of 15 years is allowed to participate in a Tunggali (sparring) competition; however, they may participate in Balangkas and Bigayan competitions.

SECTION 3: MATCHING AND PAIRING

- Single elimination: The player who loses is automatically eliminated.
- 2 out of 3 matches: The player who wins the first two matches is the winner.
- 3 out of 5 matches: The player who wins the first three matches is the winner.
- 4 out of 7 matches: The player who wins the first four matches is the winner.
- Sudden death match: The player who scores first (whether it is a full or half score) in extension matches is declared the winner.

SECTION 4 - MECHANICS OF MATCHES

- Each match will last 3 minutes for both male and female contestants.
- The first to score a killing blow (Unang Pamatay na Ulos or Isahan) within the 3 minute match time period is declared the winner and the bout is stopped.
- Point accumulation (Pagtitipon Ng Puntos or Puntosan): The contestant who scores the most points during a 3-minute match is declared the winner.

- In case of a tie and no winner is declared, a 3-minute extension match will be held after a 1-minute break.

- In case of another tie with no winner declared, another 3-minute extension will be held after a 1-minute break.

- Only two 3-minute extensions will be allowed.

- In case no winner is declared after two 3-minute extensions, a sudden death match (Unang Tama or Unahan) will be held and the first contestant who scores will be declared the winner.

- The maximum time limit for a sudden death match is 3 minutes.

- If there is still no winner, the winner is determined by a unanimous decision by the referee and the four-line judge panel based on the superiority of technique and aggressiveness.

- If a unanimous decision cannot be reached, the bout will be declared a draw (Patas) and both players will be allowed to continue to the next round or both will be declared champions (if it is the final bout).

- In case any of the players disagree to a draw decision, the administrator with the majority agreement of the referee line judges and both players may declare a winner by a coin toss.

SECTION 5: FORMAL EXERCISES COMPETITION

Balangkas (Pattern)
- Balangkas is an organized set of techniques performed by a single contestant with or without the accompaniment of music (typically native Fillipino music).

- The officiating panel for the Balangkas competition consists of three judges who are seated separately, approximately 4-feet apart in the front (white side) of the match area.

- Balangkas is a new development in the Filipino fighting arts that have been adopted from other fighting arts. However, there is no unified or standard rules for Balangkas (also called Anyo or Sayaw in other schools) in a competition. Several schools have developed their own forms.

- The maximum time limit for Balangkas is three minutes.

The criteria for scoring points in a Balangkas competition is as follows:

1. Good form: 2 points

2. Focus and concentration: 2 points

3. Power and intensity of delivery: 2 points

4. Balance, grace and rhythm: 2 points

5. Practicality of technique: 2 points

Bigayan (Give and Take)

The officiating panel in a Bigayan competition is made up of three judges who are seated separately about 4 feet apart in the front (white side) of the match area.

Bigayan is a two-man organized set of drills made up of choreographed and pre-arranged armed and unarmed offensive and defensive techniques. The early Filipino Fighting Arts practiced in this style. The maximum time limit for Bigayan is 3 minutes.

The criteria for scoring points in a Bigayan competition are as follows:

1. Realism in fight sequence: 2 points

2. Coordination and flow: 2 points

3. Focus and concentration: 2 points

4. Proper balance and distance: 2 points

5. Attitude and demeanor: 2 points

Sparring (*Tunggali*) Competition

- The officiating panel for a sparring (tunggali) competition will be a free moving referee and four stationary side judges.

- The two types of Tunggali (sparring) competitions are the individual competition and the team competition

- Individual competition: fighters go from one round to another to determine an individual champion.

- Substitution for an individual player is not allowed once the tournament starts.

- The same rules of scoring applies to both on individual and team competition.

- A team competition is essentially a competition between two groups where the winner is determined by the collective wins of the individual players

- Before a Tunggali competition, the type of match is announced as either a Unang Pamatay na ulos, Isahan (first killing blow), Pagtitipon ng puntos or Puntosan (point accumulation) match

- In team competitions, each team must be made up of the same gender

- A team must be composed of an odd number of players and consist of a minimum of three players and no more than seven players maximum.

- Players on the same team must be certified as having the same level of skill, age, and weight. This information must be certified by the team leader /manager and approved by the tournament organizers and officiating panel

- All members of the team are contestants. There will be no alternates or reserves

- A list of the team in their proper fighting order must be submitted by the team leader/manager prior to the start of the match

- There will be no substitution or shuffling of the fighting order of players after the list has been submitted

- A team will be disqualified if any substitution or shuffling of players is done by the team members or officials after the list has been submitted

- If a member of a team is disqualified (see reasons for disqualification), the whole team is disqualified from the competition

- If a member of a team is unable to compete due to an injury sustained during the match, the team may withdraw or continue with a lesser number of players. The injured player cannot be substituted by another player

- Any contestant who is not in his/her proper place when the match starts automatically loses by default

- If a coach, manager, team member or official associated with the individual player or team enters the fight area and disrupts the proceedings, the individual player or team will be disqualified

SECTION 6: LEGAL TARGETS AND SCORING

Nonlethal Area - Extremities: Upper and Lower Arms, Hands and Feet

- For purposes of a more effective and uniform system of scoring, the body will be divided into four parts, using standard medical terminology.

- Using the middle of the top of the head, draw an imaginary vertical line down the body to establish the midline of the body

- Any technique applied towards the midline is called a medial technique and any technique applied away from the midline is called a lateral technique.

- The player's left side is called the left and the player's right side is called the right.

- Using the navel, draw an imaginary horizontal line.

- Any technique applied towards the head is called the superior.

- Any technique applied towards the feet is called inferior.

- The front of the body is called the anterior.

- The back of the body is called the posterior

Legal Targets

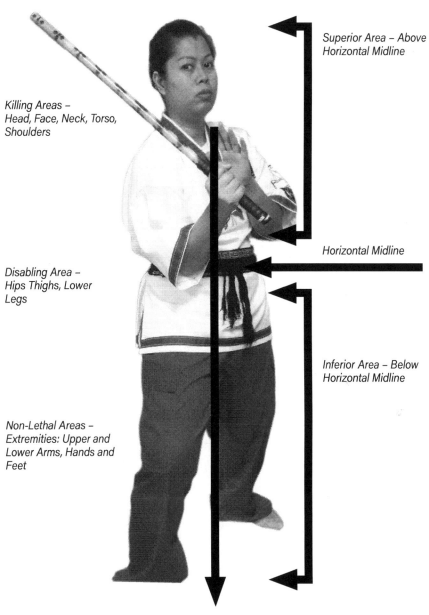

Killing Areas –
Head, Face, Neck, Torso,
Shoulders

Disabling Area –
Hips Thighs, Lower
Legs

Non-Lethal Areas –
Extremities: Upper and
Lower Arms, Hands and
Feet

Superior Area – Above
Horizontal Midline

Horizontal Midline

Inferior Area – Below
Horizontal Midline

Vertical Centerline

- Points will be awarded on the following basis:
    1. Good form
    2. Proper balance
    3. Correct distancing and timing
    4. Intensity of delivery
    5. Use of leverage and best angle of force
- Strikes and thrusts to the superior area (head, chest, sides and torso including shoulders) are considered blows to the killing area.
- Strikes and thrusts to the inferior area (hips, thighs and lower legs) are considered blows to the disabling area.
- Strikes and thrusts to the extremities (upper and lower arms, hands and feet) are considered blows to non-lethal area.
- Refer to the illustration on page 203 for legal targets.
- Any counter-strike after the referee has called a score will not count and is considered invalid.
- Simultaneous blows will not be counted as a score for either player.
- An effective technique delivered at the same time as the time-up signal will be counted into the score.
- Techniques delivered outside the fight area shall be invalid.
- Strikes to the superior killing area (head, chest, neck, sides and torso including shoulders) will be scored three points based on the following criteria:
    1. Clean and uninterrupted strike
    2. Clean follow-up technique after a clean defensive technique
    3. Clean and uninterrupted strike after the opponent is disarmed by another clean strike before the referee stops the bout. If the bout has been stopped before the strike, it will not count and may be grounds for disciplinary action against the offending player.

- Strikes to the superior killing area (head, chest, sides, neck and torso including shoulders) will be scored two points if the following criteria is met:
    1. The strike is partially blocked.
    2. The strike lacks intensity and focus.
    3. The player loses his or her balance after delivery of the strike.
- Strikes to the superior killing area (head, chest, sides, neck and torso including shoulders) will not be counted as a score if the following occurs:
    1. The strike is completely blocked or deflected before it hits the target.
    2. The player who delivers the strike is out of balance during the delivery of the strike.
    3. The player who delivers the strike is out of the fight area during the delivery of the strike.
    4. The strike is delivered after the bout has been stopped by the referee.
- Strikes to the inferior, disabling area (hips, thighs, and lower leg) will receive two points based on the following criteria:
    1. Perform a clean and uninterrupted strike
    2. Perform a clean follow-up technique after a clean defensive technique
    3. Perform a clean and uninterrupted strike after the opponent is disarmed with another clean strike before the referee stops the bout. If the bout has been stopped before the strike, it will not be counted and may be grounds for disciplinary action against the offending player.
- Strikes to the inferior disabling area (hips, thighs, and lower legs) will only be scored one point if the following criteria is met:
    1. The strike is partially blocked.
    2. The strike lacks intensity and focus.
    3. The player loses balance after delivery of the strike.

- Strikes to the inferior disabling area (hips, thighs, and lower legs) will not be counted as a score if the following occurs:
  1. The strike is completely blocked or deflected before it hits the target.
  2. The player who delivers the strike is out of balance during the delivery of the strike.
  3. The player who delivers the strike is out of the fight area during the delivery of the strike.
  4. The strike is delivered after the bout has been stopped by the referee.
- Strikes to the extremities – "non-lethal area" (upper and lower arms, hands and feet) – will be scored one point based on the following criteria:
  1. Clean and uninterrupted strike
  2. Clean follow-up technique after a clean defensive technique
  3. Clean and uninterrupted strike after the opponent is disarmed with another clean strike before the referee stops the bout.
     If the bout has been stopped before the strike, it will not be counted and may be grounds for disciplinary action against the offending player.
- Strikes to the extremities – "non-lethal area" (upper and lower arms, hands and feet) – will only be scored ½ point if the following criteria is met:
  1. The strike is partially blocked
  2. The strike lacks intensity and focus
  3. The player loses balance after delivery of the strike
- Strikes to the extremities – "non-lethal" area (upper and lower arms, hands and feet) – will not be counted as a score if the following criteria is met:
  1. The strike is completely blocked or deflected before it hits the target

2. The player who delivers the strike is out of balance during the delivery of the strike.

3. The player who delivers the strike is out of the fight area during the delivery of the strike.

4. The strike is delivered after the bout has been stopped by the referee.

Section 7: Conduct of Matches

- Prior to the start of the individual competition, the players will be divided by pool depending on the number of contestants

- Each pool must have an even number of players

- In case there is a player without an opponent, the player will be declared winner on bye and move on to the next round

- Each pool must have a maximum of 12 blue players and 12 red players

- Members of the same club or association must be distributed among the pools so they will not unjustifiably eliminate each other in the early elimination rounds

- The tournament assistant will line all the individual players of the pool in their respective sides outside the fight area

- In case of team competition, the tournament assistants will line up both teams in their proper fighting order based on the list submitted by the team leader / manager / coach

- If the tournament assistants see any discrepancy in the line-up, he will report it to the referee who will conduct an investigation and hand out the proper disciplinary action if appropriate.

- The tournament assistants will make sure that the officials' tables and stools / chairs are in their proper places

- The tournament assistants will make sure that there are at least three pairs of blue protective armors and three pairs of red protective armors and three blue sticks and three red sticks lined up on the white side outside the fight area prior to the start of the bout.

- After the players are lined up in their respective places the tournament assistant will call the tournament officials who will take their respective places

- The referee will call the attention of the players and the officials who will all stand in attention

- The officials in the officiating table, the side judges, the referee who will be standing on the far side of the fight area and the players will all face the presidential table or the flag, as the case may be

- The referee will give the preparatory command to bow (ppppuuuuggggaaaayyyy) followed by the command of execution NA and everybody will bow in unison

- The officials in the officiating table, the side judges, and the players will then turn around and face the fight area.

- The referee will give the command to bow to each other.

- The referee will then order everybody to assume their positions

- The announcer will announce the start of the competition and call the names of the first contestants who will assume their proper places in the fight area

- The tournament assistants will assist in putting on the protective armors of the first three players on both sides while the referee makes sure that they are properly fitted and secured

- The tournament assistants will step out of the fight area

- The referee will position the players and then give the signal to start the bout.

- When a scoring blow is delivered the referee will call the score and simultaneously stop the match and order both players to their respective starting positions

- In a clear and concise manner the referee will announce the score giving credit to the player who scored and advise the scorekeeper

- Time will not be stopped

- If it is a first killing blow match (Unang Pamatay na ulos or ISAHAN), the referee will announce the winner and stop the match

- If it is a point-accumulation match (Pagtitipon ng puntos or PUNTOSAN), the referee will order both players to continue the match

- If the referee sees a foul or unacceptable technique, the referee will stop the match and order both players to their respective starting points then give his decision whether it is a warning, point deduction or disqualification - time will not be stopped if it is a warning or point deduction

- After the scorekeeper is advised the referee will order both players to continue or stop the match and declare the winner as the case may be

- If the referee sees an injury, he will stop the bout and advise the timer to stop the time and display a black banner

- The referee will call the medical officer to check and decide on the injury

- The referee will confer with the side judges to determine who or what caused the injury and what action to take

- If the match is continued, the referee will order both players to assume their starting positions, signal the timer to resume time and display a white banner and continue with the match

- If the match cannot be continued, the referee will declare the winner or declare a draw as the case may be.

- Only in individual competition will players who are done with their match be allowed to leave their line

- In team competition, if a member of a team is disqualified, the whole team is disqualified and ordered to leave the line and the opposing team will be declared the winner

- In team competition, if a member of a team is injured and unable to continue the match, the team will be allowed to continue if it wishes, however, the team will have one slot vacant. Substitution is not allowed whether on the current or subsequent matches.

- Anybody who leaves the line after the match has started will be declared loser by default.

SECTION 8: TABLE OF JUDGMENT

Victory of Red

1. Red Red Red Red - Victory of Red
2. Red Red Red Blue - Victory of Red
3. Red Red Red Draw - Victory of Red
4. Red Red Draw Draw - Victory of Red

Victory of Blue

1. Blue Blue Blue Blue - Victory of Blue
2. Blue Blue Blue Red - Victory of Blue
3. Blue Blue Blue Draw - Victory of Blue
4. Blue Blue Draw Draw - Victory of Blue

Victory of Either

1. Red Red Blue Blue - Victory of either depending on referee
2. Red Red Blue Draw - Victory of red depending on referee
3. Blue Blue Red Draw - Victory of blue depending on referee

Draw

1. Draw Draw Draw Draw - Draw
2. Red Draw Draw Draw - Draw
3. Blue Draw Draw Draw - Draw
4. Red Draw Draw Blue - Draw

Section 8-A: Referee's Hand Signals

Pugay sa harapan (facing the officiating table officials and players salute to the flag

Pugay sa bawat isa: Players salute each other.

Simula: At the start of the contest, referee brings both open hands to each other.

Tigil: Stop motion used to signal players to separate from each other.

Tuloy: Resume. Referee brings open hands to each other.

Taposna: It is over. Referee motions players to separate from each other and then motions them to starting positions.

Magkasabay na palo: Simultaneous blows. No point for either player. Referee brings fist to each other.

Walang nakitang puntos: Indicates that the referee did not see any scoring blow, and referee covers both eyes.

Walang puntos: No point awarded. Referee waves open hands downwards crossing each other.

Tigil ang oras: Stop time referee makes a time out signal as he looks at the timer. Black flag is raised.

Tuloy ang oras: Continue time referee points to the clock and timer puts up white flag

Decision: Referee blows whistle long and hard to request judges' decision.

Draw: Referee extends both hands downward with palms facing forward.

Red foul major infraction leading to disqualification: Referee strikes right arm on left arm indicating red foul on blue and then in a harsh motion points red index finger outwards.

Blue foul major infraction leading to disqualification: Referee strikes left arm on right arm indicating foul on red and then in a harsh motion points blue index finger outwards.

Right hand red

Puntos: Red full point. Refree brings right arm 90-degrees up.

Kalahating Puntos: Red half point. Referee brings right arm perpendicular to the ground.

Panalo: Red winner. Referee brings right hand straight up.

Labas: Red outside. Referee points right hand to the border line.

Red foul minor infraction that may lead to red's point deduction. Referee brings right hand up, waves it in circles overhead.

Left Hand Blue

Puntos: Blue full point. Refree brings left arm 90-degrees up.

Kalahating Puntos: Blue half point. Referee brings left arm perpendicular to the ground.

Panalo: Blue winner. Referee brings left hand straight up.

Labas: Blue outside: Referee points left hand to the border line.

Blue foul minor infraction that may lead to blue's point deduction: Referee brings left hand up, waves it in circles overhead.

Section 8-B: Judge's Flag Signals

Right Hand Red

Red Full Score: Flag Pointed Upward, Right Arm 90 Degrees

Red Half Score: Flag Pointed To The Right Side

Red Winner: Flag Pointed Upward Right Arm Straight

Red Foul: Waving Flag In Circle Over- Head

Red Outside: Flag Being Pointed To The Outside Line

Left Hand Blue

Left Full Score: Flag pointed upward left arm 90 degrees

Left Half Score: Flag pointed to the left.

Left Winner: Flag pointed upward left arm straight.

Left Foul: Waving flag in circle overhead.

Left Outside: Flag being pointed to the outside line.

Did Not See Score: Flags covering the eyes.

Dead Blows: No score. Flags pointing to each other.

No Score: Flags being crossed twice, pointing down.

Draw: Flags crossed overhead

Section 9: Fouls, Violations, And Penalties

Minor Violations

Refusal to engage opponent or stalling for time and continuous stepping out of fight area penalty:

- 1st offense: Warning
- 2nd offense: Point deduction
- 3rd offense: Disqualification from competition

Dropping of fighting stick penalty

- 1st offense: Warning
- 2nd offense: Point deduction
- 3rd offense: Disqualification from competition

Turning back to opponent penalty:

- 1st offense - warning
- 2nd offense - point deduction
- 3rd offense - disqualification from competition

Hitting prohibited targets designated non-legal targets

- 1st offense: Warning
- 2nd offense: Point deduction
- 3rd offense: Disqualification from competition

Major Violations:

- Refusal to obey instructions of tournament officials
  Penalty: Disqualification and disbarment from future competitions

- Unsportsmanlike conduct unbecoming a martial artist, such as swearing, profanity, throwing of stick or any part of protective gear and other unruly behavior
  Penalty: Disqualification and disbarment from future competitions

- Unsportsmanlike conduct unbecoming a martial artist by an official, coach or another member affiliated to the player, such as swearing,

profanity, entering the fight area and other unruly conduct
Penalty: Disqualification and disbarment from future competitions of the player and/or the team

- Actions and techniques that are dangerous and injurious to the opponent, the officials and the spectators
  Penalty: Disqualification and disbarment from future competitions

Section 10: Injuries

Injury Sustained in the Course of the Fight

- If the injury is caused by the injured party, and he is not able or allowed by the medical officer to continue the fight, the other player may be declared the winner by default and allowed to move on to the next round.

- If the injury is caused by the other player, and the injured party is not able or allowed by the medical officer to continue the fight, the player who caused the injury is disqualified and the injured party is declared a winner but will neither be allowed to continue the fight or allowed to move on to the next round. That particular bout will be eliminated from the competition.

- If the cause of the injury cannot be determined and both players are not able or allowed to continue the fight by the medical officer, both players will be eliminated from the competition.

- If the cause of the injury cannot be determined and the injured player is not able or allowed to fight by the medical officer, the other player will be declared the winner and allowed to move to the next round.

- If the cause of the injury cannot be determined and both players are able to continue the fight ,the bout will continue, but if time runs out and no player is ahead on points, the referee with the unanimous concurrence of the line judges may declare a winner based on superiority of techniques and aggressiveness.

- If the cause of the injury cannot be determined and time runs out and no one is ahead on points and superiority of techniques and aggressiveness , the bout will be declared a "draw" and both players will be eliminated from the rest of the competition.

- The referee must solicit the opinion of the medical officer and only the medical officer can certify if an injured player is able to continue the fight.

- If the injury cannot be alleviated by the medical officer with first aid in 5 minutes, the rest of these provisions will apply.

- The referee shall call a time out to resolve questions about injuries.

APPENDIX 1

REPUBLIC ACT 9850 (ARNIS LAW)

This teacher's training handbook was written to be in accord with the Phillipines Republic Act No. 9850 (Arnis Law), and the authors felt it fitting to include the law as this book's foreword.

Begun and held in Metro Manila on Monday, the 27th day of July 2009:

REPUBLIC ACT (9850)

An act declaring Arnis as the national martial art and sport of the Phillippines. Being enacted by the Senate and House of Representatives of the Philippines in Congress assembled:

SECTION 1. It is the policy of the State to inculcate patriotism, nationalism, and appreciation of the role of national heroes and symbols in the historical development of the country. Furthermore, the State must give priority to education, science and technology, arts and culture, and sports to foster patriotism and nationalism, accelerate social progress, and promote total human liberation and development.

SECTION 2. Definition of Arnis - Arnis, also known as Eskrima, Kali, Garrote and other names in various regional languages, such as Pananandata in Tagalog; Pagkalikali, Ibanag; Kabaroan and Kalirongan, Pangasinan; Kaliradman, Bisaya and Didja, Ilokano, is an indigenous Filipino martial art and sport characterized by the use of swinging and swirling movements, accompanied by striking, thrusting and parrying techniques for defense and offense. This is usually done with the use of one (1) or two (2) sticks or any similar implements or with bare hands and feet also used for striking, blocking, locking and grappling, with the use of the same principle as that with the canes.

SECTION 3. Arnis is hereby declared as the Philippine National Martial Art and Sport. The official adoption of Arnis as the National Martial Art and Sport shall be promulgated by inscribing the symbol of arnis in the official seal of the Philippine Sports Commission and by making it as the first sport competition to be played by participating teams on the first day in the annual Palarong Pambansa. The Philippine Sports Commission shall be the lead agency to implement the provisions of this Act.

SECTION 4. The Department of Education, the National Commission for Culture and Arts and the Philippine Sports Commission shall promulgate the necessary Rules and Regulations to carry out the provisions of this Act.

SECTION 5. Any provision of law, decree, executive order, rule or regulation in conflict or inconsistent with the provisions and/or purposes of this Act is hereby repealed, amended or modified accordingly.

SECTION 6. This Act shall take effect fifteen (15) days after its complete publication in the Official Gazette or in at least two (2) newspapers of general circulation.

Approved, This Act, which is a consolidation of Senate Bill No. 3288 ad House Bill No. 6516, was finally passed by the Senate and House of Representatives on October 14, 2009.

APPENDIX 2

THE MATAW GURO ACADEMY

The *FMA Informative* has covered the Mataw-Guro Association since it conception which was on July 31, 2010. The idea behind the Association was superb and a great aspect to move towards any style of the Filipino martial arts. It was to teach the very foundation that can be found in all Filipino martial arts styles and systems. To the *FMA Informative* understanding the basics are the beginning, pertaining to, or forming a base, an essential ingredient, principle, procedure, etc. Fundamentals are serving as, or being an

essential part of, a foundation or basis, a basic principle, rule, law, or the like, that serves as the groundwork of a system. And a core is the central, innermost, or most essential part of anything.

The formation of the Mataw-Guro Association was done to teach the basics of the Filipino martial arts. What are the basics of the Filipino martial arts? Is it 3 strikes, or 5 strikes, 7 strikes or 12 strikes is it the way one blocks? In empty hand is it an inward, outward, downward, and upper block? Are the blocks circular or angular? In the body movement in stances are they triangular, angled, circular, or horizontal / vertical? In the execution of leg movements for kicking and sweeping what is the concept for balance, power and speed?

All are basics to all the Filipino martial arts. It is the way they are explained, taught and the principles in the execution and philosophies that make them different. All Filipino martial arts are great in their own respect. What makes each art better than the other? Nothing really, it is what the receiver (student / practitioner) perceives and what their body adapts and coordinates to and what

in their mind; is the best art for them personally. What is the Mataw-Guro Association trying to do? It is attempting to bring together the Filipino martial arts practitioners which realize and wants to teach the basics, fundamentals, the core of the Filipino martial arts so the student will understand the structure and essentials and then be able to move on with this knowledge to a style which will fully benefit them and they will adapt and excel in, becoming the best they can be.

The Mataw-Guro Association has no ranking all are believed to be equal in their goals to teach the basics of the Filipino martial arts. Of course, there is the Founder (Louelle Lledo) who had the dream of establishing such an Association, and Officers of the Association which are appointed, to bring about organizational value, and to represent and guide the Association in the goal it was established for. Well as in all Associations, Organizations, and Federations, etc. there are problems, which cover a variety of things, unfortunate that it happens. And some Associations, Organizations, and Federations fold and disappear into history.

Louelle Lledo has continued in his dream of the Mataw-Guro providing the education of the Filipino martial arts. So, starting Phase 2, Lou has established the Mataw-Guro Academy which consists of practitioners that teach the program to the original mindset that was and has been the goal of the Mataw-Guro. *—Steven K. Dowd, publisher of The FMA Information. This article is excerpted in part from issue #215.*

Forming a Foundation

July 31, 2010 practitioners gathered for the 6th East Coast Filipino Martial Arts Gathering. This was not the typical gathering for practitioners from throughout the United States attended to share their knowledge. The theme of the gathering was that teachers would demonstrate, teach and promote what is called the "ABC's" of their art, the basics that make up their style of Filipino martial arts.

The need for a term to convey the meaning of a high standard teacher of the martial arts in the academy environment became necessary. The term Mata-Guro, coined from Mataas na Guro was suggested. But the word did not have the "ring" or the "back- bone" required. The term was later changed to Mataw, which was coined from mataas ang tanaw (high standard). Thereafter, the term Mataw-Guro or teacher of high standard came about. The title Mataw-Guro (knowledgeable teacher or master teacher) thereafter was chosen as the rank of the highest level in the academy.

With the title and the need to form an association of educators agreed upon, it became imperative to set down the qualifications and requirements to be a member. This task fell on the shoulders of Louelle Lledo. He selected the teachers he knew who have a successful program of instruction.

It was on February 12, 2010, the Mataw-Guro Association was formally established, composed of the 17 founding members and 2 posthumous members.

On March 6, 2010 at the Joy Tsin Lau Restaurant, 1026-2B Race St., Philadelphia, PA., where the United Fellowship of Martial Artists was holding their first Hall of Fame Banquet. With the cooperation of Dr. John Lee the head of the United Fellowship of Martial Artists, Punong Mataw-Guro Louelle Lledo was able to commence forming a foundation for his dream of uniting the teachers of the Filipino martial arts.

In this a category for the main body of Mataw-Guros (Master Teachers) was formed and recognized.

To note again in the Mataw-Guro Association the practitioners are designated with the same title, and the reason is that all are equal in the development of the Mataw-Guro Association which the Association will (once fully established) be comprised of Filipino martial arts practitioners that can properly teach the ABC's (basics) of the Filipino martial arts.

Well since that time, many things have transpired, members some have departed and some have joined. The members that have departed had their reasons and their journey for the future took them in a different directions, some members have become inactive and just are names on the Mataw-Guro Association list.

First Step: Establishing the Basics

Punong Mataw-Guro Louelle Lledo and Mataw-Guro Andy Sanano realized that the Filipino martial arts are taught in an almost roundabout manner.

All Arnis de Mano schools or styles have one thing in common – the way the art was being taught. Training starts by facing the opponent and blocking his strike. This training goes on until the student becomes an adept. Most instructors believe that this is the best and the only way to teach the fighting art - by actual ex- change of blows from day one. A training session starts with engagement and ends with engagement. "No pain, No gain" seemed to be the principle on which learning Arnis de Mano revolved. Another "sorry" state of training the "old-fashioned" way, without the use of padded sticks or protective gear, is the injuries the trainees sustained. Aesthetics and good form were being sacrificed, for the sake of injuring the opponent to make him give up. More and more "one-technique fighters" and less and less martial artists are being produced. As less and less martial artists, are being produced, less and less good teachers are also being produced.

Punong Mataw-Guro Louelle Lledo and Mataw-Guro Andy Sanano did not develop "new" techniques or a "new" style. What he did was to "rearrange" the way the techniques were taught. The first step was to plot a course of study, which will cover all the aspects of the Filipino martial arts and set the stage for upward evolution to an exciting and aggressive but safe modern fighting art. He separated the "unarmed" techniques from the "armed" techniques, but based the training on a common platform. Comparing the techniques will show that they are one and the same. The only difference is that "unarmed" techniques use the empty hands and the "armed" techniques use a weapon. Whether the weapon is a single stick, a double stick, a knife, an alternative weapon, or even the empty hands, the maneuvers are the same.

Their next step was to break down the maneuvers into their most basic elements. To achieve this purpose, the maneuvers, were classified as "basic" and "progressive." "Basic" meant executing the maneuvers in forms and drills.

"Progressive" meant applying the maneuvers to various different situations or as Lledo says "situational application."

Another term he uses, when referring to "basic" is "foundation." The foundation included such matters as stances, breathing, footwork, basic strikes, basic thrusts, one-man drills and one-man forms, such as the classical maneuvers, and the Salpukan (Impact Training) and the Palaisipan (mental game) or shadow fighting.

Application of techniques, whether in two-man drills or two-man forms were called "Progressive training". The drills or forms may be in the manner of Bigayan or Palitan (semi-free style sparring) or Sabakan (free-style sparring or engagement).

After laying out the program, Punong Mataw-Guro Louelle Lledo and Mataw-Guro Andy Sanano worked on the "nitty-gritty" elements. They broke down each maneuver to its most minute element and explained the techniques in detail. Starting with stance, they differentiated stance of execution from preparatory stance and explained the proper utilization of the stance in relation to the center of gravity and proper breathing. As a natural consequence, good form and aesthetics came about. With good form, proper use of body mechanics, leverage and direct application of force came naturally.

Punong Mataw-Guro Louelle Lledo then selected classical maneuvers that were common in almost all the styles and schools, such as the kruzada, the single and double sinawali, the figure of eight, the redonda, the abaniko, the rompida, the sungkiti and other variations. He broke down and explained the basic patterns of linear motion into diagonal, vertical and horizontal; circular motion into clockwise and counter-clockwise; the basic strikes into forehand and backhand; the basic thrusts into overhand and under-hand; and the disarming techniques into arm turn and arm twist. He designed warm-up and cooling down exercises from ordinary calisthenics into stick-fighting specific and oriented movements. He instituted one-man, two-men and even multiple-opponent drills. The emphasis of his training method was to make every technique a "simple reaction."

During the on-set of the Mataw-Guro Association four books were written and published tat explained and gave samples of the basic, principles and concepts the Arnis de Mano which were to be taught at Mataw-Guro events.

Filipino Martial Arts Education Arnis de Mano, as developed, and written by Mataw Guro Louelle Lledo, Jr., and Mataw Guro Andy Sanano, Jr., is the result of several years of teaching, and hard work. In addition to the years of individual training and study that the authors have invested towards their personal development in the Filipino martial arts, they have worked hard in collaboration to present this work, the product of their intellectual endeavor.

They wrote and produced the four Teachers' Training Handbooks that have been merged into this greater volume. The first handbook is the *Filipino Martial Arts Education: Teacher's Training Handbook*, which served as the foundation of the next two volumes. *The Teacher's Training Course Handbook: Principles of Classical Maneuvers,* and *Teacher's Training Handbook: Balangkas Ng Abecedario,* were the second and third book in the series. The fourth book that completes this new edition is called *Karunungang Lihim Ng Arnis De Mano,* and *Sports Arnis De Mano Tournament Rules and Regulations.* Together, these volumes comprise the greater edition which is intended to help develop teachers, and students in the official martial art of the Philippines – Arnis De Mano.

The Philippine Government has selected Arnis De Mano as the official martial art of the country. Arnis is not only martial arts training, but an excellent presentation of tradition, culture and Philippine history. Integrating Arnis De Mano in the public educational system will be of great benefit to teachers and students in the continuity and strengthening of knowledge of Philippine history, culture and traditions. The expectation of this textbook is to help develop the ability of teachers and students to present a consistent educational curriculum across all of the traditional systems and schools of Arnis De Mano while respecting the variations among them.

In recent years, practitioners of the Filipino martial arts have become increasingly active and visible in their arts. This publication is offered to all instructors

and students and may it serve as a tool for the growth and development of Filipino Martial Arts Education.

Mataw-Guro Academy – Organized and Founded December 19, 2015 at the Pinoy Dragon Zikdokan Sikaran Amara Arkanis Martial arts Academy, Jackson, New Jersey. Mataw-Guro Marlon Hudak was host and assisting the presenters. It was hosted by Mataw-Guro Marlon Hudak Mataw Guro Academy, Director and faculty for Amara Arkanis system.

The founding occasion was celebrated with a workshop gathering of Mataw-Guro members. Senior students of different systems, friends and supporters. It was a workshop of the abecedarios or abcs of the basic fundamental of the different styles and systems of the Mataw-Guro Academy faculties.

Mataw-Guro Louelle C. Lledo started the occasion with the commonality of blocks, slashs, thrusting and the combination of the three techniques. He also explained the only two basic strikes of armed and unarmed martial arts, forehand and backhand or vice versa that you can strike anywhere you want with these two techniques. He showed how it was expanded by Maestros of the past to twelve angles of situations.

Then the next presenter was Mataw-Guro. Oliver Garduce of Punite Combatant Zikdokan Sikaran Amara Arkanis Canada, showing the ABCs of his system, the middle range combat.

After Mataw-Guro Walter Crisostomo followed with the basics of their Ultimate Crisostomo Eskrima system. He showed their famous witic pitic or abanico largo to corto.

After him came Mataw Guro Rommel Guiveses of World Sikaran Amara Arkanis New York, showing Sikarans basic kicks and how the develop them using their partners.

It ended with the awarding of Black sash 1st degree to Richard Calogero Glover, 8th Degree black and red sash to Mataw-Guro. Marlon Hudak, NJ. Mataw-Guro Oliver Garduce Canada and Rommel Guiveses NY. The workshop ended with a lot of Filipino food for dinner for all participants, courtesy of Mrs. Flora Lledo and Mataw-Guro Kathlou Lledo and Mataw-Guro Marlon Hudak.

Mataw-Guro Andy Sanano, Dr. Christopher Viggiano and Dr. Mark Wiley had an emergency to attend to, so were unable to attend the last minute.

The Comfirmation of the Mataw-Guro Academy

Mataw Guro Academy Workshop "Save a Life" February 13, 2016, Traditional Wing Chun Fu Academy Princeton Place Shopping Center 3747 Church Rd., Mt Laurel, NJ.

Seminar / Workshop "Save a Life" of a martial arts brother and friends life. Mataw-Guro Felipe Penales of Mataw-Guro Association Amara Arkanis System, having dialysis in the Philippines. Tis event is for donation for Mataw-Guro Felipe Penales which was presented by the Mataw-Guro Academy, Traditional

Wing Chun Kung Fu Academy North America HQ. Sword Stick Society International, World Sikaran Brotherhood USA. Also two-fold this event is the final gathering to establish and promote the Mataw-Guro Academy. The second phase of the Mataw-Guro Association.

The event began with Dr. Christopher Viggiano of Sword Stick Society International showing and ex- plaining foot work maneuvers, with stick and bladed weapons functions and the forehand and backhand principles. This was followed by Sigung Keith Mazza of the Traditional Wing Chun Kung Fu Academy demonstrating the circular empty hand art with a detailed expla- nation. Then Grandmaster Bob Martin of Sword Stick Society International demonstrated and explained the bumblebee circular empty hands and body movements and maneuvers.

This was followed by Mataw-Guro Marlon Hudak Pinoy Dragon Amara, and Mataw-Guro Rommel Guiveses of World Sikaran Brotherhood explaining and demonstrating the stretching and Sikaran basic kicking exercises. Followed by Dr.Mark Wiley of Integrated Eskri- ma International demonstrating and explaining how to secure the gate and control the ranges of stick fighting.

Then Mataw-Guro Walter Crisostomo of Ultimate Eskrima Pinakatay Segida Crisostomo system showed the basic of their witik pitik or fanning abaniko corto system. Guro Jhun Occidental continued with his Grandmaster Tabuada 90* maneuvers power left and right basic blocks. Next was Mataw-Guro Andy Sanano of Trece Humpas Sanano System with his combination Punyo offensive and defensive techniques.

To bring a final part of the event Mataw-Guro Lou Lledo explained the basic fundamental forehand and backhand strikes with fraction half strikes Combate Heneral with half fraction strikes in between, adding to this he explained the three ranges or defense and offense.

Mataw-Guro Association - to - Academy

After the seminar / workshop the Mataw-Guro faculty members, which consist of the different styles which are taught at the Mataw-Guro Academy FMA Education programs, sat down to discuss. Program's and plans of the academy.

It was decided that the Academy will be composed of a Dean, to oversee and plan programs of activities for the Academy, And an Assistant Dean as the Administrative Officer.

The Mataw-Guro Association was formed to merges the different styles and systems in America to design, establish and approve a basic fundamentals for teaching Filipino martial arts Education, specially Arnis de Mano to be presented to the Philippine Government, Sports and Education Commission, as the Mataw-Guro Association contribution to the Arnis de Mano development, grassroots, schools, Colleges and Universities Physical Education Programs. It is the only Association that can accredit and evaluate the Filipino martial arts based on the four classical or traditional systems common to all the different major styles in the Philippines.

Mataw-Guro Association Membership does not qualify you to teach the program and get a Mataw-Guro Academy Faculty Certificate and Authority to teach the (copyrighted) Mataw-Guro Academy Programs.

Mataw Guro Academy, is the second part after the creation of the Mataw-Guro Association.

To join the Mataw Guro Academy, you must join the Mataw Guro Association and learn to teach the Mataw-Guro Academy FMA Education Programs. Programs are categorized into Levels one, two and three.

For Questions Contact Punong Mataw-Guro Lowelle Lledo:
inquiry@matawguro.com

APPENDIX 3

THE 1ST WORLD FMA UNITY SEMINAR

How It Began and What Transpired

The Filipino martial arts are at a turning point. The once secretive fighting arts are now Youtube sensations and available at a seminar or two near you nearly every weekend. With all the open access and popularity these arts now have, they are changing and morphing into systems that look like FMA used to look. And these days there are just so many masters and GM that it's hard to keep track of. In the old days, there was a master. Let's use Remy Presas as a nice example. He spread the modern version of arnis into the

Philippine school systems and to martial artists throughout the word. When he was alive, there was Modern Arnis. Now that he has passed, we have hundreds of masters under him now claiming new system names and grandmaster titles. The same thing happened when Angel Cabales passed away, and again when Antonio Ilustrisimo passed away; and the list goes on. I am not judging here if this is "good" or "bad," as that all depends where you stand. But what has occurred is a near impossibility of tracking systems lines, lineages, and a fragmentation of the art that is as large as the art itself.

Philippine Organizations Unite

In the Philippines, Raymond S. Velajo has been head of the government recognized Arnis Philippines for decades. He has tried to unite the different systems and masters under one organization, with different levels of success. Arnis Philippines, with the support of Philippine Olympic Committee, Philippine Sports Commission, Philippine Department of Culture and Tourism, held a

gathering of masters in San Juan City in 2015. In attendance were Raymond Velayo, Shishir Inocalla, Dr. Mark Wiley, Bambit Dulay, Rodel Dagooc, Victor Cusi, Pepito Robas, Frank Aycocho, Earl Bruce Villanueva, De La Rosa, Alex Co and Dada Shiveshananda. The meeting was covered by Jean Russel V. David, reporter for *The Manila Times*.

At the gathering, in addition to celebrating the 14th memorial of the passing of Prof. Remy Presas, Velajo announced a new organization as a branch of Arnis Philippines, to help unite Arnis globally. That new arm is called Arnis Pederasyong Internasyonal, Inc. (i-ARNS).

i-ARNIS

The aim of i-Arnis is to give recognition to special individuals for Arnis skills acquired or contributions done for the propagation of Arnis as a martial art and sport by classifying practitioners with a sports Arnis Grading System. This grading system is specifically designed for Arnis to standardize levels for all its practitioners. It will set up specific requirements to ensure that the rank given is in accordance to the criteria established to determine the level of expertise of the practitioner.

This system will also protect the origins of the different Arnis styles and their masters, thereby protecting the history of the styles. Arnis masters shall be given the proper stature and honor they truly deserve. International ambassadors were established to promote FMA Culture & Tourism, beginning with Datu Shishir Inocalla and Dr. Mark Wiley. Inocalla and Wiley were then asked to make plans to unify FMA and to begin this by promoting the first World FMA Unity Seminar combining the associations of the Philippines (mentioned above) and the unifying FMA association in North America: The Mataw Guro Association.

Mataw Guro Association & Academy

According to Louelle Lledo, who founded the Mataw Guro Association in 2010, "It's not the style but the Mataw Guro that makes all the difference. There is no better art, only a better person. The art is the person and the person is the art." This is an important notion because most people form or join an association to get an elevated rank. But the Mataw Guro Association was formed with a different view in mind.

Conscious of the need of developing enthusiasm, interest, and dedication in the field of Filipino Martial Arts Education, and in order to act as guardians of the noble and beneficial aims of Arnis de Mano and compelled by Lledo and Andy Sanano's desire to establish an association which shall be the rallying point of all teachers of Arnis de Mano as a Filipino Martial Arts Education, the Mataw Guro's hereby mutually agree to unite and associate themselves for such a purpose. There is no rank and file among teachers, only the shared title of "Mataw Guro" or master teacher.

The Mataw Guro Association was formed to merges the different styles and systems in North America by designing, establishing and disseminating a basic fundamental for teaching Filipino martial arts education. The aim is to support Republic Act 9850 (arnis as national martial art and sport of Philippines). The Mataw-Guro Association legacy is to contribute to FMA development through grassroots efforts, schools, and the physical education programs within colleges and universities. It is the only Association that can accredit and evaluate the Filipino martial arts based on the four classical or traditional systems common to all the different major styles in the Philippines.

The Association then formed the Mataw Guro Academy wherein it appointed faculty for legitimate teaching of the FMA education fundamentals programs. The Academy consists of Mataw Guros from different styles: Llouelle Lledo (Amara Arkanis), Andy Sanano (Sanano Martial Arts), Emmy Querbin (Sikaran), Dr. Christopher Viggiano (Shen Wu Dao), Bob Martin (United Force Martial Arts), Dr. Mark Wiley (Integrated Eskrima), Marlon Hudak

The Lecturer

MG Bob Martin, MG Richard Lundy, MG Rommel Guiveses, MG Marlon Hudak, MG Oliver Garduce, MG Walter Crisostomo, MG Christopher Viggiano, MG Louelle Lledo, MG Andy Sanano and MG Mark Wiley.

Mataw-Guro Academy Filipino Martial Arts Arnis De Mano for Education

(Pinoy Dragons), Walter Crisostomo (Ultimate Eskrima), Rommel Guiveses (Sikaran), Spencer Gee (Pananandata), and Oliver Garduce (Kombatan).

1st World FMA Unity Seminar

Datu Shishir and Dr. Wiley spent months coordinating efforts in the role as International Ambassadors of FMA Culture. Shishir began teaching in Macau and Korea and Guanzhou. Wiley rallied his support behind the Mataw Guro Association, for which he serves as Senior Adviser and PA State Ambassador, and joined them in promoting seminars in Pennsylvania and New Jersey.

Then a date was selected for the First Word FMA Unity Seminar to be held in Montgomery Township, PA on June 4-5, 2016. This became the forerunner in a series of FMA Unity seminars now sweeping the USA, Canada, and Brasil. This first event was hosted by Dr. Mark Wiley and supported by the Mataw Guro Association, i-ARNIS, Arnis Philippines, Philippine Dept. of Tourism, Philippine Sports Commission, Philippine Olympic Committee, Integrated Eskrima International, World Sikaran Brotherhood, Society of Black Belts of America, Arnis Kali Maharlika, National Committee for Culture and Arts, and Tambuli Media.

Over 80 participants, over two days came from all over the US and Canada to learn the basic course in FMA Education as set by the Mataw Guro Academy. Instructors included masters from many styles all coming together to share their common basics.

The Seminar was presided over by Mataw Guro Association Founder and CEO Mataw Guro Louelle Lledo and by the MGA International Coordinator, MG Andy Sanano. Several Mataw Guros were an active part of the event including MG Bob Martin, MG Rommel Guiveses, MG Marlon Hudak, MG Oliver Garduce, MG Walter Crisostomo, MG Abel Colon, MG Richard Lundy, MG Dr. Christopher Viggiano, Keith Mazza as well as our host MG Dr. Mark Wiley and our leaders, MG Louelle Lledo and MG Andy Sanano. Many of the Mataw Guros offered training sessions making this a very successful event. Special guest and iArnis representative, Datu Shishir Inocalla also shared his knowledge and brought his support.

The overall purpose of the seminar was to strengthen FMA Education as is the Mission of the Mataw Guro Association. In particular, the seminar was offered in active support of RA 9850, establishing Arnis as the national sport and martial art of the Philippines. This MGA event was endorsed by the Philippine Sports Commission, the Philippine Department of Tourism, the National Culture and Arts Association and the Philippine Olympic Committee. A consortium of these organizations and agencies has awarded the Mataw Guro Association a Certificate of Recognition for the presentation of this first World FMA Family Unity Seminar. And each participant received a Certificate of Attendance with all association logos as support.

World FMA Family

With the huge success of the First World FMA Unity Seminar, Datu Shishir Inocalla and Dr. Mark Wiley, as the International Representatives of iArnis, and backed by Arnis Philippines president Raymond S. Velayo, set up a new unity website, www.WorldFMAFamily.com to be a place where everyone involved in this new movement toward unity can share their events and news. Have a look, join us on Facebook, and support Unity in FMA, not more division.

APPENDIX 4

GLOSSARY OF TERMS

Developed and arranged by the World Sikaran Brotherhood of the Philippines and approved by the Institute of National Language, Department of Education in 1969, for use in Filipino martial arts Education. Re-printed with permission of WSBP Grandmaster Meliton C. Geronimo and his executive and technical assistant Emmanuel es Querubin.

General Terms

Art of stick fighting	Arnis de Mano *
Art of foot fighting (fighting art of the Filipino farmer)	Sikaran
Also considered English terms due to common usage	
Sikaran practitioner	SikaraNista
Arnis practitioner	ARNISista/Arnisador
Sikaran attire	Kasuotang pang Sikaran
Arnis attire	Kasuotang pang Arnis
Ancient Art	Sinauanang sining
System of self-defense	Pamamaraan ng pagtatanggol sa sarili
Modern sport	Makabagong palakasan
Local fighting system	Pamamaraan ng pampurok na pakikilaban
Science	Agham
Concentrated forceful exhalation	Bun-yaw (Kiai in Japanese)
Intrinsic inner strength (life force)	Nimbo (Chi in Chinese or Ki in Japanese)
Full contact	Ubodkaya
Skin (touch) contact	Sayadlang

Focus	Paslik (formal)
Focus	Pokus (coloquial)
Ju-jitsu	Ditso
Local wrestling	Buno (Dumog / Barog)
System using sweeping techniques	Palis-palis
System using slapping techniques	Tapik-tapik
System using fanning techniques	Pamaypay (abaniko)
System using weaving techniques	Pahabi (sinawali)
Hand to hand techniques	Mano-mano
Natural weapons	Sandatang likas
Manmade (artificial) weapons	Sandatang likha
Optional (Alternative) weapons	Sandatang pinili
Rigid (stiff) weapons	Sandatang matigas
Pliable (flexible) weapon	Sandatang sunod-akma
Casting (projectile) weapons	Sandatang panudla
Batangas local street fighting system	Babag
Weaponry	Pananandata

Rigid/Stiff Weapons	Sandatang Matigas
Single cane / sword	Solo baston/espada
Single fixed blade knife	Solo daga/punyal/balaraw patalim
Fan /butterfly/knife	Balisong
Double cane / sword	Doble baston / espada
Double knife	Doble daga / punyal
Cane sword and knife	Espada Y daga
Eight (8) foot to ten (10) foot' long pole	Tungkod
Five (5) foot to six (6) foot medium pole	Tungkli
Palm stick (4"-5")	Kudlit
Palm board (4" diameter)	Panampal
Tonfa	Basnga
Nunchaku	Basbit

Sickle	Karit
Reaper	Dulos
Hook	Gantso / kawit
Fan	Abaniko / Pamaypay
Axe	Palakol (when used for hacking)
Trident (Sai in Japanese)	Salapang
Flexible/Pliable Weapons	**Sandatang Sunod Akma**
Bandana/handkerchief	Pandong / panyo
Chain	Kadena
Belt	Sinturon
Sash	Paha
Whip	Latigo
Projectile/Casting Weapons	**Sandatang Panudla**
Firearm	Baril
Slingshot	Tirador
Blow-gun	Sumpit
Pop-gun	Sumpak
Bow and arrow	Pana
Spear	Sibat
Throwing dart / knife	Tunod
Throwing star	Suligi
Throwing axe	Puthaw (smaller axe used for throwing)
Strong non stop attack	Hampas kalabaw (colloquial)
Strong non stop attack	Walang puknat (formal)
Strong non-stop attack	Sagasa (slang)
Fist fight	Suntukan (colloquial)
Fist fight	Panuntukan (formal)
Fist fight	Bakbakan (slang)
Free for all	Labo-labo
Anything goes	Bara-bara
No holds barred	Sali lahat
Fraction system	Sistemang praksiyon

Deception	Linlang
Heads and tails	Puno't dulo
Association	Samahan
Brotherhood	Kapatiran
Club	Kapisanan
Society	Katipunan
Member	Kasapi
Team	Koponan
Board	Lupon
Basic technique	Batayang pamamaraan
Elementary technique	Panimulang pamamaraan
Intermediate/progressive technique	Maunlad na pamamaraan
Advance technique	Mataas na pamamaraan
Quadrant	Kabahaging apatan
Striking configuration	Paraan ng paghablig
Round / Circle (shape)	Bilog
Circular (direction)	Paikot
Linear (direction)	Paguhit
Oval /oblong	Habilog
Standing triangle	Tatsulok
Reverse triangle	Baligtad na tatsulok
Square	Parisukat
Rectangle	Parihaba
Figure of eight	Pa-otso
Anterior / Front	Harapan
Posterior / Back	Likuran
Horizontal midline	Kalagitnaang pahalang
Vertical midline	Kalagitnaang patayo
Upper/Superior (from the waist up)	Itaas
Lower/Inferior (from the waist down)	Ibaba
Upward (from the feet going up)	Pataas/Pamayong

Downward (from the head going down)	Pababa/Buhat araw
Inward	Papasok (going in towards vertical midline)
Outward	Palabas (going out from vertical midline)
Salutation when one Sikaran player meets another Sikaran player.	Po

Position	**Katayuan**
Duty	Tungkulin
Instructor/teacher	Guro
Head instructor/teacher	Punong-guro
Master	Dalubhasa
Master instructor teacher	Dalubhasang guro
Master teacher	Matawguro
Head Master Teacher	Punong Matawguro
Expert	Batikan
Grandmaster	Punong dalubhasa/Pantas/Paham
Founder	Nagtatag/Tagapagtatag
Heir	Tagapagmana
Successor	Kahalili
Referee	Tagapasiya
Judge	Tagahatol
Administrator	Tagapangasiwa
Arbiter	Tagapamagitan
Score keeper	Tagatala
Timer	Tagatakda
Announcer	Tagapahayag
Tournament assistant	Katulong sa paligsahan
Reporter	Tagaulat
Medical Officer	Tagalunas
Second	Alalay
Champion	Hari

Winner	Panalo
Loser	Talunan
Manager	Tagapamahala

Training Equipment — Kagamitang Pansanay

Training hall	Bulwagang sanayan (Bothoan)
Punching board	Dalindingan ng suntok
Punching bag	Supot suntukan
Speed stick	Pabitin
Speed ball	Matuling bola
Skipping rope	Luksong lubid
Foot stretcher	Pambanat ng paa
Weight training	Sanayan na may pabigat/barbel
Protective Armor	Baluting pananggalang
Head gear	Kupya/Baluting pang-ulo
Gloves/hand guard	Guwantes/Baluting pang-kamay
Shin Guard	Baluting pang-lulod
Groin protector	Baluting pang-bayag
Mouthpiece	Pananggalang pambibig

Commands — Utos

Salutation	Pagpugay
Standing salutation	Nakatayong pagpugay
Kneeling bow	Nakaluhod na pagpugay
Ready to bow	Handang magpugay
Preparatory command to bow	Pugay
Command of execution	Na
Report	Mag-ulat
Move	Galaw
Start	Simula
Break	Tigil
Separate	Hiwalay
Stop it is over	Tapos na
Foul	Maruming paraan
Disqualify	Alis/ talsik

Expelled	Tanggal
Point	Puntos
Half-point	Kalahating puntos
No point	Walang puntos
Draw/tie	Patas
Simultaneous blows	Sabayan
Continue	Tuloy
Rest	Pahinga
Starting position	Lugar ng simula
Return to position	Balik sa pinanggalingan
Fall in	Magtipon
In columns	Maghanay
Dismiss	Tiwalag na
Turn around	Umikot
Move forward	Sumolong
Move backward	Umurong
Move sideward	Urong sa tagiliran
Move diagonally	Urong ng pahiwid
Kneel down	Lumuhod
Sit down	Maupo
First killing blow	Isahan (unang patama)
Sudden death match	Unahan
Point accumulation match	Puntosan
Pairing match	Tapatan
Round-robin match	Paikotan
Handicap	Partida
Shift stance	Magpalit ng tayo
Transfer weight	Maglipat ng bigat
Stances	**Tayo**
Natural stance	Tayong likas
Inverted toe stance	Tayong papasok
Parallel stance	Tayong kaagapay
Open toe stance	Tayong palabas

Cat stance	Tayong patiyad
Crane stance	Tayong tagak
Hourglass stance	Tayong piki
Forward stance	Tayong pasulong
Back stance	Tayong paurong
Straddle stance	Tayong pasaklang
Diagonal stance	Tayong pahiwid
Square stance	Tayong parisukat
Ready stance	Tayong handa
Preparatory stance	Tayong paghahanda
Fighting stance	Tayong panlaban

Postures	**Tindig**
Front facing	Tindig na Paharap
Side facing	Tindig naPatagilid
Half-front facing	Tindig naPalihis
Diagonal facing	Tindig na pahiwid
Back facing	Tindig na patalikod

Break Falls	**Tamang Pagbaksak**
Forward	Bagsak paharap
Sideward	Bagsak patagilid
Backward	Bagsak patalikod
Roll	Magpagulong
Roll with the punch	Sumunod sa puwersa

Steps	**Lakad**
Step forward	Lakad pasulong
Step sideward	Lakad patagilid
Step backward	Lakad paurong
Step diagonally forward	Lakad palihis pasulong
Step diagonally backward	Lakad palihis paurong
Half step	Kalahating hakbang
Double step	Magkasunod na hakbang
Sliding step	Padulas na hakbang

Slide forward	Dulas pasulong
Slide sideward	Dulas patagilid
Slide backward	Dulas paurong
Slide diagonally forward	Dulas palihis pasulong
Slide diagonally backward	Dulas palihis paurong
Target	**Tudlaan**
Top of the head	Tuktok
Forehead	Noo
Back of the head (Nape)	Batok
Temple	Sintido
Bridge of the nose	Balingusan
Upper lip	Nguso
Chin	Baba
Nostrils	Ilong
Jaw	Panga
Eyes	Mata
Ears	Taynga
Neck	Leeg
Adam's apple	Lalamunan
Windpipe	Lalaugan
Jugular vein	Bena sa leeg
Carotid artery	Ugat sa gilid ng leeg
Clavicle	Balagat
Armpit	Kilikili
Heart	Puso
Solar plexus	Sikmura
Abdomen	Tiyan
Lower abdomen	Puson
Testicle base	Bungol
Testicle	Bayag
Spine	Gulugod
Kidney	Bato
Liver	Atay

Floating ribs	Huling tadyang
Coccyx	Kuyukot
Wrist	pupulsuhan
Elbow	Siko
Back of the hand	Umbok ng kamay
Fingers	Daliri sa kamay
Toes	Daliri sa paa
Forearm	Bisig o braso
Leg or foot	Paa
Knee	Tuhod
Hollow of knee	Alak-alakan
Knee cap	Takip tuhod
Instep	Balantok
Shin	Lulod
Thigh	Hita
Achilles heel	Bala-kong
Natural Weapons	**Sandatang Likas**
Top of head	Tuktok
Forehead	Noo
Back of head (nape)	Batok
Open hand	Bukang kamay
Closed fist (hand)	Ikom na kamay
Spear-hand	Dalibat
Fore-knuckle	Kamayri / Kobra
Knife-hand	Kamayga
Ridge-hand	Kamaylid
Palm	Palad
Palm heel	Sakonglad
Thumb and fore and middle finger pincher	Panipit
Fore-fist	Kamao
Bottom-fist	Kamaypok
Back-fist	Kamaykod

Inner forearm	Losig
Outer forearm	Lasig
Elbow	Siko
Leg or foot	Paa
Knee	Tuhod
Instep	Balantok
Heel	Sakong
Edge of foot	Limpyak
Ball of foot	Bilogan
Sole	Talampakan
Shin	Lulod
Man-Made (Artificial) Weapons	**Sandatang Likha**
Sword	Espada
Saber	Sable/eskrima
Cane/stick	Baston
Dagger	Patalim/balaraw/daga/punyal
5 inches palm stick (Yawara in Japanese)	Kudlit
5 inches palm stick with middle ridge	Tribuson
Palm disk	Plapla
Fan knife/Butterfly knife	Balisong
Sickle	Karit
Hook	Gantso/kawit
Reaper	Dulos/panggamas
Axe	Palakol
Spear	Sibat
Blowgun	Sumpit
Popgun	Sumpak
Bow (only)	Busog
Arrow (only)	Palaso
Bow and arrow	Pana
Slingshot/sling	Tirador

8' Long pole	Tungkod
5' to 6' foot pole	Tungkli/Pingga/Bangkaw
Sai (Trident)	Salapang
Tonfa	Basnga
Nunchaku (sectional staff)	Basbit
Throwing dart/knife	Tunod
Throwing star	Suligi
Takedowns/Throws	**Ibagsak/Itapon**
Sweeping	Pawalis
Reaping	Pagapas
Tripping	Papatid
Pulling	Pahila
Pushing	Patulak
Scooping	Pasalok
With the hands	Pamamagitan ng kamay pakamay
With the feet	Pamamagitan ng paa papaa
With the hips	Pamamgitan ng balakang – pabalakang
Arm push – leg pull	Tulak ng braso – hila ang paa
Kick behind knee	Sipa sa alak-alakan
Over the shoulder throw	Hagis pasang araro
Body slam	Hampas sa lupa / balibag
Hip throw	Hagis pasang sako ng bigas
Joint Reversal	**Pagsaliwa Ng Hugpungan**
Arm turn (turning wrist)	Pilipit
Holding technique	Pamamaraan ng pagpigil
Elbow lock to break	Pagbali ng siko
Head lock to break	Pagbali ng leeg
Punching Techniques	**Pamamaraan Ng Pagsuntok**
Straight punch	Sunwid
Rising punch	Suntas
Downward punch	Sunba

Lunge punch	Sunlong
Reverse punch	Sunbalik
Roundhouse punch	Sunkot
Hook punch	Sunwit
Uppercut punch	Sikwat
Vertical punch	Suntamay
Corkscrew (turning fist 180-degrees) punch	Suntribuson
Pushing punch	Sunlak
Jabbing punch	Sundot
Blocking punch	Sunlag
Alternate punch	Sunlinan
Thrusting Techniques	**Pamamaraan Ng Pagtusok**
Fore knuckle thrust	Tusok ng kamayri/kobra
Spear hand thrust	Tusok ng dalibat
Elbow Techniques	**Pamamaraan Ng Pagsiko**
Upward elbow strike	Sikowat
Forward elbow strike	Sikorap
Sideward elbow strike	Sikolid
Backward elbow strike	Sikokod
Downward elbow strike	Sikoba
Striking Techniques	**Pamamaraan Ng Paghablig**
Knife-hand strike	Habligga
Inward strike	Habliggang papasok
Outward strike	Habliggang palabas
Forward strike	Habliggang paharap
Downward strike	Habliggang pababa
Reverse hand	Habliggang tumbalik
Backhand strike	Habligwa
Ridge-hand strike	Habliglid
Palm heel strike	Habliglad
Sideward strike	Habliglad patagilid
Upward strike	Habliglad pataas

Back-fist strike	Habligkod
Bottom-fist strike	Habligpok
Inner forearm strike	Habliglosig
Outer forearm strike	Habliglasig
Roundhouse fore knuckle strike	Habligkamayri
Kicking Techniques	**Pamamaraan Ng Pagsipa**
Thrust kick	Padyak
Stomping kick to knee	Padyak ng Kalabaw
Front kick	Siparap
Front thrust kick	Padyak na paharap
Front snap kick	Pilatik
Instep	Pilatik ng balantok
Ball of foot	Pilatik ng bilogan
Side thrust kick	Padyak patagilid
Foot edge	Padyak patagilid ng limpyak
Heel	Padyak patagilid ng sakong
Diagonal thrust kick	Padyak na pahiwid
Back thrust kick	Padyak na patalikod / Sipang Kabayo
Hooking heel kick	Sipawit
Crescent kick	Sipakan
Twisting (reverse crescent) kick	Sipang baliswa
Oblique front thrust heel kick	Sipang alanganin
Spinning heel kick	Biyakid
Roundhouse kick	Sipakot
Instep	Sipakot ng balantok
Ball of foot	Sipakot ng Bilogan
Shin	Sipakot ng lulod
Jumping kick (from standing still)	Damba
Jumping front kick	Dambarap
Jumping side kick	Dambalid
Jumping diagonal kick	Dambawid

Jumping spinning heel kick	Dambang biyakid
Jumping hooking kick	Dambawit
Jumping roundhouse kick	Dambakot
Flying kick (from running start)	Dagit ng Agila
Double kick	Sipang sabay paa
Knee kick	Tuhurin
Front leg kick	Sipa ng harapang paa
Rear leg kick	Sipa ng likurang paa
Blocking kick	Sipalag
Faking kick	Lansipa
High kick	Sipang mataas
Middle kick	Sipang gitna
Low kick	Sipang mababa
Other Forms Of Attack	**Ibang Paraan Ng Pansabak**
Ferocious wild buffalo (only found in the Philippines)	Tamaraw
Head butt	Sibasib/suwag ng tamaraw
Monkey	unggoy (smaller type of wild monkey that attacks viciously without warning)
Monkey attack	Daluhong ng unggoy
Wild fowl	Labuyo
Fighting cock	Panabong
Type f fighting cock	Bulik
Flapping of wings of a wild fowl	Pagaspas ng labuyo
Fighting cock frontal assault	Salpok ng bulik
Break (arm/ribs)	Baliin
Split (head/skull)	Biyakin
Gouge off (eyes)	Dukitin (ang mata)
Squeeze (testicles)	Pisain
Squeeze (neck)	Sakalin
Deflecting Techniques	**Pamamaraan Ng Panglihis**
Blocking Techniques	**Pamamaraan Ng Pagsalag**

Flapping of wings by wild fowl	Pagaspas ng labuyo
Downward block	Salag Buhat Araw (old SIKARAN)
Downward block	Salagba
Inner forearm	Salagbang losig
Outer forearm	Salagbang lasig
Reverse arm	Salagbang tumbalik
Inward block	Salagsok
Reverse arm	Salagsok na tumbalik
Outward block	Salagbas
Inner forearm	Salagbas ng losig
Outer forearm	Salagbas ng lasig
Reverse arm	Salagbas na tumbalik
Upward block	Salag na Pamayong (old SIKARAN)
Upward block	Salagtas
Reverse arm	Salagtas na tumbalik
Knife-hand block	Salagga
Vertical	Salaggang patayo
Upward	Salaggang pataas
Downward	Salaggang pababa
Circular	Salaggang paikot
Double	Salaggang dalawang kamay
Palm heel block	Salaglad
Upward	alaglad pataas
Downward	Salaglad pababa
Sideward	Salaglad patagilid
Ridge-hand block	Salaglid
Backhand block	Salagwa
Dropping block	Salaglag
Scooping block	Salaglok
Pressing block	Salagdiin
Pushing block	Salaglak
Pulling block	salaghil
Grabbing block	Salagma

Roundhouse block	Salagkot
Sweeping block	Salaglis
Augmented forearm block	Salagsig
Elbow block	Salagko
Punching block	Salagtok
Wedge block	Salaglang
X block	Salagkis
Upward	Salagkis pataas
Downward	Salagkis pababa
Combination block	Salaglong
Knee block	Salaghod
Kicking block	Salagpa
Crescent kick block	Salagkan
Hooking block	Salagwit
Choreograhped Pattern (Formal Exercise)	**Balangkas**
Basic pattern	Batayang balangkas
Bell (4 –direction) pattern	Balangkas ng kampana
Intermediate pattern	Pani-langkas
Progressive pattern	Mau-langkas
Foreign pattern	Balangkas na Banyaga
Weapons pattern	Balangkas ng sandata
Cane/stick	Baston
Sword/live blade	Buhay na talim / Kalis / itak
Dagger	Balaraw/punyal/patalim
Long pole	Tungkod/pingga
Structured pattern	Isinaayos na balangkas
Free expression pattern	Sariling damdamin na balangkas
Free style pattern	Sariling pamamaraan na balangkas
Sparring	**Labanan**
Basic technique	Batayang pamamaraan
Foundation	Saligan/Haligi

Pre-arranged one step sparring	Isang hakbang na bigayan
Pre-arranged three steps sparring	Tatlong hakbang na bigayan
Semi-free sparring	Palitan
Free-style sparring	Sabakan (formal)
Free-style sparring	Upakan (slang)
Contest/tournament fighting	Paligsahan / Tunggali

ABOUT THE AUTHORS

Louelle C. Lledo, Jr.,
Amara Arkanis International

Experience, Awards and Positions Held in The Martial Arts:

- Accredited International Referee, Judge, and Arbitrator by the World Union of Karate-do Organizations (WUKO).

- Trained regional and national Karate players (Philippine Karate Association) in the World Union of Karate-do Organizations (WUKO) style of international competition.

- PKA's youngest international referee trained regional and national officials in the WUKO style of international officiating.

- Supervising agent-in-charge of the City of Manila's Civil Intelligence and Security Unit (CISU) branch of the National Intelligence and Security Agency (NISA).

- Trained members of the City of Manila's Civil Intelligence and Security Unit in Unarmed Combative Arts.

- Defensive Tactics and Unarmed Combative Arts Teacher HQ Integrated National Police Training Command, National Capital Regional Training Center.

- Unarmed Combative Arts Teacher of the National Bureau of Investigation Training Academy.

- Defensive Tactics Teacher of the 1st Air Division and 304th Security Squadron of the Philippine Air Force.

- Defensive Tactics Teacher of the NCO Academy, Department of the US Army, Fort Dix, New Jersey, USA.

- Monitoring Officer of the Philippine Sports Commission (Governing body of amateur combative sports in the Philippines) for Karate-do, Judo, Taekwondo, Arnis de Mano, and Archery.

- Director and Head Teacher of the Filipino martial arts Educational Development Program, College of Sports Physical Education and Recreation, Cavite State University, Indang, Cavite, Philippines.

- Cavite State University Head Coach of the University Combative Sports Varsity Teams.

- Sports Commissioner for Combative Sports of the State, Colleges, and Universities Athletic Association (SCUAA) Southern Tagalog, Region IV.

- Director and Technical Consultant of the National Association of Schools Karatedo Organizations of the Philippines (NASKOPHIL).

- Consultant, Advanced Resource for Martial Arts Educational Development (ARMED).

- Director, Advanced Resource for Martial Arts Studies (ARMAS).

- Ambassador Plenipotentiary of the Department of Tourism's Office of Philippine Indigenous Fighting Arts.

- Author of Martial Sport Arnis Official Handbook for Physical Education of Cavite State University.

- Author of the following textbooks: AMARA ARKANIS, The Fighting Art of the Mandirigma and AMARA ARKANIS Sistemang Praksiyon Filipino martial arts Education.

- Co-author of two Filipino martial arts education, teacher's training handbooks.

- Director and Co-founder of Swordstick Society International.

- Renshi, International Goju-ryu Karate-do Federation.

- Tagapagmana and Punong-guro of Bernarte Brokil Sistemang Praksiyon.

- Founder of Amara Arkanis Sistemang Praksiyon Martial Arts Education.

- In 2012, he was promoted to the 9th Degree Red and White Belt (Registration No. 326) in the World Sikaran Brotherhood.

- Inducted to the Action Martial Arts Magazine Hall of Fame in 2003 as Grandmaster of the Filipino martial arts, recognized in 2004 for the Propagation and Preservation of the Filipino martial arts, and recognized in 2009 for Bridging the Gap Between the Filipino and Chinese Fighting Arts.

- Featured writer of the Educational Depot Column in the Filipino martial arts Digest, an internet magazine devoted to the Filipino martial arts published by Steven Dowd in Fallon, Nevada, USA.

- Founder and chief executive officer (CEO) of the Matawguro Association of Filipino martial arts Education for Arnis de Mano.

- Recipient of the United Fellowship of Martial Artists 2010 Hall of Fame

- Honored as martial arts author of the year for his book *AMARA ARKANIS, Fighting Art of the Mandirigma.*

- In 2012, he became the recipient of the Award For Meritorious Service To Philippine Culture from Senator Miguel Zubiri, author of the Republic Act 9850, Indang Mayor Bienvenido Dimero, Dr. Davinia Chavez of Cavite State University, and Dr. Alejandro Dagdag, Executive Director of the Integrated College of Physical Education and Sports.

- In 2013, he was appointed New Jersey Sate director of the World Sikaran Botherhood of the Philippines.

- In 2013, the United Fellowship Of Martial Artists (UFOMA) awarded him the Award of Superiority in recognition as an Outstanding International Master Teacher of the Filipino martial arts Education, and for co-authoring the book Arnis De Mano Filipino martial arts Education. He was also vested the Award for Scholarly Achievement.

www.amaraarkanis.com

Andy Sanano, Jr.,
Sanano Martial Arts System

- *Grandmaster Sanano Martial Arts System

- *Serve as a Reserve Lieutenant Police Special Respond Team aka SWAT (16years).

- *Retired Military, United States Air Force , Intercontinental Ballistic Missiles Specialist

- Education: Doctor of Martial Arts Philosophy (Ph.D), University of Martial Arts Studies, Indiana, Indianapolis, U.S.A., 2014

- Birth Date: February 7, 1951

- Born with fraternal sister, Marylou Sanano

- Place of Birth: Legazpi, Albay, Philippines

- Andy Sanano was adopted by his biological aunt and uncle in 1961 when his parents passed away.

- In 1969 his family emigrated to the United States of America.

- In 1956 He learned the rudiments of stick fighting from his grandfather and uncles who were the caretakers of their family art, the Trecehampas System of Arnis de Mano. His adversary in training were the banana trees and the tall cogon grass while walking in the field. Little did he know that he was being prepared to someday take over the family art.

- When the family moved to Manila he sought training in the fighting arts. He joined the Sikaran class At the Sikaran Brotherhood of the Philippines gymnasium in Pasay City. His insatiable appetite for the fighting arts led him to join the Pering Cruz Dojo, where the curriculum included Karate, Judo, Ju-Jitsu (Jujutsu) and Arnis de Mano, where his growing up "play in the fields" started to have meaning.

- After receiving his Blackbelt at the age of 18 his adopted parents brought him and his fraternal twin sister to San Francisco, California. While in San Francisco Kempo was added into his martial arts repertoire.

- For 16 years he was a Reserve Lieutenant with the Rapid City, South Dakota Police Department, assigned to the Special Response Team (SRT) sometimes referred to as SWAT in other Police Agencies.

- Later on he joined the US Air Force and was eventually stationed in Ellsworth Air Force in South Dakota. He retired after 20 years.

- While in the service, he trained in all the martial arts that came his way such as: Tae Kwon Do, Uechi-Ryu Karate, Shotokan Karate, White Crane Kung Fu, Aikido and other weapon arts. To honor the family art he consolidated all the systems he learned and formed the Sanano Martial Arts System (SMAS) with numerous affiliates all over the United States.

- His expertise in the martial arts received several gold medals in competitions and tournaments.

- His instructions emphasizes individual development of self discipline, awareness and respect for self and other as well as the values and attitudes necessary for the proper application of the Martial Arts.

- He teaches, "Learn To Fight Not To Fight."

His Other Awards Are:
- USA Hall of Fame, 2014 Atlanta, Georgia,

- World Sikaran Brotherhood of Canada Hall Of Honor 2014 Winnipeg, Manitoba, Canada

- United Fellowship of Martial Artist Hall of Fame, 2013 Philadelphia,PA

- 1st Philippine Martial Arts Hall of Fame, 2012 Manila, Philippines

- Action Martial Arts Magazine Hall of Honor, 2009 Atlantic City, NJ

- World Karate Union Hall of Fame, 2008, Tannersville, Pennsylvania.

- USA Martial Arts Hall of Fame 2004, Milwaukee, Wisconsin

- Canada Sikaran Arnis Hall of Fame 1995, Winnipeg, Manitoba, Canada

- In 2013 The United Fellowship of Martial Artists (UFOMA) conferred on him the Award of Superiority in recognition as an "Outstanding International Master Teacher of the Filipino Martial Arts Education" and for co-authoring the book, ARNIS DE MANO FILIPINO MARTIAL ARTS EDUCATION. He was also vested the "Award for Scholarly Achievement".

- In 2012 However he considers the Award for "Meritorious Service to Philippine Culture", bestowed to him by Senator Miguel Zubiri, Author of the Arnis Law, Indang, Cavite Mayor Bienvenido Dimero, Dr. Davina Chavez, President of Cavite State University and Dr Alejandro Dagdag, Executive Director of the Integrated College of Physical Education and Sports the "Crowning Glory" of his martial arts career.

- In 2012 he was promoted into the 9th Degree White and Redbelt by Grandmaster Meliton C. Geronimo, Sr., World Sikaran Brotherhood of the Philippines.

- Recipient of the "Bukal ng Karunungan Award" from Cavite Governor Remulla, Cavite Mayor Bienvenido Dimero, Cavite state University Vice President and Martial Arts Program Director Dr Alejandro Mojica on April 14, 2012.

- 2010 The United States Fellowship of Martial Artist with headquarters in the East Coast vested on Andy an "Award of Excellence for the Propagation and Development of the Filipino Martial Arts in the United States."

- Living Legend, 2014, Atlanta, Georgia

- Distinguished Sikaran Instructors Award, 2014 Winnipeg, Canada

- International Grandmaster of the Year, 2012 Manila, Philippines

- Grandmaster of the Year, 2008 Tannersville, Pennsylvania

- Martial Artist of the Year, 2000 Rapid City, South Dakota

- Top Referee Award, 1999, Winnipeg, Manitoba, Canada

- Outstanding Instructor of the Year, 1988, Gillette, Wyoming

Martial Arts Championship Awards:
- Grand Champion, 2001, 2002, 2003, Northern Plains Martial Arts Open, North Dakota
- Grand Champion, 1996, 1997, 1998, Cheyenne Open Karate Championships, South Dakota
- Grand Champion, 1997, 1998, Black Hills Kicker Championships in South Dakota
- Grand Champion 2001 Martial Arts Open, Rapid City
- Grand Champion, 1992, Winnipeg, Manitoba, Canada

Positions:
- In 2011 Andy Sanano co-authored with Louelle Lledo the Teacher's Training Handbook no.1 entitled: "The Fundamentals of Arnis De Mano, and The Teacher's Training Handbook No. 2 entitled: Fundamentals of Abecedario, Handbook No. 3 entitled: Principles of Classical Maneuvers and KALI (Karunungan Lihim) ng Arnis De Mano.
- Grandmaster Sanano is a Certified Instructor for the Defensive Tactics Institute Inc. He has provided instructions for numerous Law Enforcement Agencies, Security Officer Teams and Government Agencies around the region including:
  - Rapid City Police Department, South Dakota
  - Cheyenne River Sioux Tribal Police of Eagle Butte, SD
  - Rapid City Regional Hospital Security Team
  - Rapid City Rushmore Mall Security Team
  - Presbyterian Hospital of Albuquerque, NM Security Team
  - Army Corps of Engineers, Seattle District Rangers, Washington
  - Army Corps of Engineers, Portland District Rangers, Oregon
  - Army Corps of Engineers, Pittsburgh District Rangers, Pennsylvania

- Probation officers of Santa Barbara, California
- Probation officers of Inyo County, California
- Indian Health Service Community Health Representative Training Program (CHR)

Program (CHR)

- CHR Anchorage Alaska
- CHR Rapid City South Dakota
- CHR Phoenix, Arizona
- CHR Lawton, Oklahoma,
- CHR Radio City, Tennessee
- CHR Stillwater, Oklahoma
- One of the founding member of Mataw Guro Association for Filipino Martial arts Education (Mataw Guro means master teacher).
- In 2010 Andy Sanano and other Filipino Martial Arts Teachers formed the Mataw Guro Association Filipino Martial Arts Education for Arnis de Mano, of which he is the International Coordinator.
- He is the Grandmaster of the Trecehampas family tradition of Arnis de Mano and Awayan (Ah-wah-yahn) (the art of fighting).
- He is the Mataw Guro International Coordinator
- He is the World Sikaran Brotherhood USA Regional Director, and Florida State Director.

Advisor, Board of Director

- Black Belt Society Of America, Member
- Stick & Sword Society International Representative/Ambassador
- United Fellowship of Martial Artist, Senior Advisor.
- KIDO Martial Arts, Board of Director
- The 7th Directions School of Martial Arts, Board of Director
- World Karate Union, Board of Director
- Northwest Bushinkai Aikido, Board of Director

- Verbal Judo, Senior Advisor
- USA Martial Arts Hall of Fame, South Dakota State Representative
- 10th degree in Trecehampas Arnis
- 10th degree in Awayan
- 9th degree in Black Belt in World Sikaran Brotherhood and Arnis
- 8th degree Black Belt in Arnis Alambra style
- 5th degree Black Belt in Shotokan Karate
- 5th degree Black Belt in Filipino Combat Judo

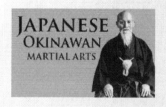

64585730R00158

Made in the USA
Charleston, SC
01 December 2016